# Activating Lunar Alchemy

The Mystical Art of Transmuting Your Emotional Pain Into Spiritual Abundance

Sydney Francis

First published by Ultimate World Publishing 2024
Copyright © 2024 Sydney Francis

ISBN

Paperback: 978-1-923123-94-6
Ebook: 978-1-923123-95-3

Sydney Francis has asserted her rights under the Copyright, Designs and Patents Act 1988 to be identified as the author of this work. The information in this book is based on the author's experiences and opinions. The publisher specifically disclaims responsibility for any adverse consequences which may result from use of the information contained herein. Permission to use information has been sought by the author. Any breaches will be rectified in further editions of the book.

All rights reserved. No part of this publication may be reproduced, stored in or introduced into a retrieval system, or transmitted in any form, or by any means (electronic, mechanical, photocopying, recording or otherwise) without the prior written permission of the author. Any person who does any unauthorized act in relation to this publication may be liable to criminal prosecution and civil claims for damages. Enquiries should be made through the publisher.

**Cover design:** Ultimate World Publishing
**Layout and typesetting:** Ultimate World Publishing
**Editor:** Rebecca Low
**Cover image copyrights:** Teo Tarras-Shutterstock.com

Ultimate World Publishing
Diamond Creek,
Victoria Australia 3089
www.writeabook.com.au

# Testimonials

"As a student of the Moon work for three years, I have manifested a life full of meaning, achievement, and purpose. Sydney's guidance and knowledge have offered an adytum within the sanctuary of discovery and actualization, uniting the Moon's cycles with the internal cadence of self."

Angie Allen, author of *Drake's Flight, Balance Oracle,* and *Poetry Exposed*

"Since working with the moon cycles and creating my Moon Wheels, I have found myself more in touch with my true passions as well as nature. It has helped me become clearer in my purpose while identifying what my next steps are. I am able to see patterns that I can reflect on, change, and make adjustments as I grow and move forward in my goals and dreams. I would recommend this work to everyone at any stage of life and spirituality. It is amazing what we can accomplish when we put our thoughts into it!"

**Franchisca Rinaldi**

"I have been using Lunar Alchemy for several years now. I have tried various goal-setting or personal development systems in the past, but this process stands out to me because of its balanced and intuitive approach. Through following this process, I have gained clarity and insight which has helped me grow as a person and achieve meaningful outcomes in all areas of my life."

**Scott Moore**

"The Moon Work taught by Sydney Francis is truly life-changing and something I highly recommend."

"Sydney has a wealth of knowledge and infuses her teaching with great insight and perspective that only years of study can provide. Sydney has a rich understanding of many different schools of study and is able to teach complex concepts with ease and grace. The moon work offers insights into the workings of our inner world and allows access to more hidden complex shadow traits—all in a framework that is both insightful and easy to use. I have personally experienced shifts in my awareness, perspective and behavior in ways that have allowed me to view and challenge my limiting beliefs. This has resulted in more clarity, insight and the ability to make positive changes in my life. The framework appears simple, yet as I continue to work with the moon wheel and the phases of the moon, I find the knowledge and personal growth continues to expand and go deeper. You can take this work as far as you like—from setting intentions to delving into deep work manifesting your deepest desires. It's exciting to see intention and desire manifest in the physical world. The moon work is a wonderful tool for spiritual growth for both the novice and advanced practitioner."

**Taz Chaudry, co-author of**
***Belonging: Secrets to Soothe the Soul***

"The Moon work is great. I made a lunar wheel, focusing largely on my job/work since that's what was occupying my mind at the time. It was really interesting. For instance, I could really see and feel how, for every goal I have, there is an equal and opposite thing to release...sort of like a yin and yang. So, you can work the goal from both sides, according to the prevailing Universal energy. I feel empowered!"

**Kate Kirby**

# Dedication

To my friend Michelle, who introduced me to *seeding the Moon* and many other magical insights.

# Contents

| | |
|---|---|
| Introduction | 1 |
| CHAPTER 1: The Magic of Pain | 11 |
| CHAPTER 2: The Magic of the Moon | 23 |
| CHAPTER 3: The Magic of Dreaming | 43 |
| CHAPTER 4: The Magic of Desire | 53 |
| CHAPTER 5: The Magic of Creativity | 65 |
| CHAPTER 6: The Magic of the Moon Wheel | 77 |
| CHAPTER 7: The Magic of Seeding the Moon | 87 |
| CHAPTER 8: The Magic of Supportive Action | 99 |
| CHAPTER 9: The Magic Mirror | 115 |
| CHAPTER 10: The Magic of Transmutation | 127 |
| CHAPTER 11: The Magic of Attention | 141 |
| CHAPTER 12: The Magic of Listening | 155 |
| CHAPTER 13: The Magic of Decision | 165 |
| About The Author | 175 |
| Acknowledgements | 177 |
| References | 181 |
| 2 Offers With Calls To Action | 183 |
| Speaker Bio | 187 |
| End Notes | 189 |

# Introduction

*"The Moon symbolizes the reflected light of the subconscious."* – Paul F. Case, The Tarot

*"Magic is the art of changing consciousness at will."*
– Dion Fortune

**Why Activating Lunar Alchemy?**

Often, the magical is hidden in the practical. I consider the Moon work of *Activating Lunar Alchemy* to be practical work, like gardening, that reveals the magic of our beingness through our kinship to the cosmic order and the rhythmic cycles of the Sun and Moon. When you attune to the timing of the rhythm of the Moon, you begin to feel a oneness with Creation.

# Activating Lunar Alchemy

This work is about being intentional with your life and being proactive toward your dreams and desires. You do this in conscious attunement to the Moon's rhythm in order to optimize timing and the flow of energy. *Activating Lunar Alchemy* is an easy-to-follow four-step ritual process that you do in synchronicity with the four main phases of the Moon: New Moon, First Quarter, Full Moon, and Last Quarter.

The Moon is, of course, important. Yet, this work is about attuning to the Earth's rhythms and electro-magnetic field or aura, influenced by the Moon. As a citizen of planet Earth, you and your aura, too, are influenced by the subtle energy of the Moon's rhythm. This process isn't about connecting with something outside of yourself but rather attuning to and becoming aware of a rhythm that's operating within you.

There are many benefits to engaging in this Moon process, including:

- Actively creating a life of meaning and purpose
- Tapping into your inner guidance and intuition
- Gaining clarity and direction
- Developing and expressing your authentic self
- Transforming damaging emotional patterns and limiting beliefs into sources of strength and abundance
- Increasing your self-love, self-acceptance, and self-awareness
- Becoming empowered and unstoppable

### *Actively create a life of meaning and purpose*
In doing this Moon work, you're doing the work of creating your best life. Your creative process is conducted in attunement with the Moon's rhythm through a weekly ritualistic process designed

# Introduction

to get you in harmony with the Moon. There are four categories of actions guided by the energy of the four main phases of the Moon Cycle: listening and 'seeding the Moon,' taking supportive action, observing and self-reflection, and releasing or letting go. By following this rhythmical process, you gently transform your life into one of meaning and purpose.

## *Tap into your inner guidance and intuition*
By attuning to the Moon cycle using the Moon Wheels, you connect deeply with your dreams and desires. You also get into contact with the subconscious obstacles that keep you from achieving your dreams and desires. As you do this self-reflective process of attuning to the Moon and your own energy, you increase your self-awareness, inner guidance, and intuition.

## *Gain clarity and direction*
The most frequent praise I get for this process is that it brings its practitioners clarity and direction. Knowing what you want is one of the most important components of creating what you want. Clarity gives you spiritual direction. In other words, it shows which way to move forward and what actions to take in order to achieve your dreams and desires.

## *Develop and express your authentic self*
Part of this process is self-reflection, which helps you discover yourself and define your authenticity. As you practice this Moon work over a period of time, you'll witness your life transforming for the better. Your life will reflect increasing alignment with your authentic self.

## Activating Lunar Alchemy

### *Transform damaging emotional patterns and limiting beliefs into sources of strength and abundance*

One of the most important aspects of this practice happens in alignment with the Last Quarter Moon. This is where you release and shed your old patterns, limiting beliefs, emotions, and behaviors. Releasing old patterns, habits, and behaviors is necessary to sustain healthy growth.

In my experience, many people don't follow their dreams and desires because of emotional obstacles and subconscious patterns. As soon as you begin taking action toward your big dreams, whatever you believe and feel about yourself regarding achieving that dream is going to come up. Whether you call them limiting beliefs, programs, or emotional patterns, these inner obstacles are very compelling and attempt to convince you to stay in your comfort zone, where you can stay safe and stop pursuing your dreams and desires. One of the most important aspects of this process is recognizing and shedding these old beliefs and patterns. This frees you to feel better and create fulfillment and abundance in all areas of your life.

### *Increase your self-love, self-acceptance, and self-awareness*

I need to stress the importance here that this is a practice that's conducted over time. The cyclical process of aligning with the Moon cycle will help you develop self-love, self-acceptance, and self-awareness. But this may not happen after one Moon cycle; the magic doesn't work that way. Healing your life to live your dreams, grow, and have fulfillment is an ongoing process of creativity and internal reflection. Your life mirrors your energy. What you consciously and unconsciously project about yourself is the basis for what you experience in life. When you engage in this Moon work, you become self-aware and empowered by your strengths, gifts, passions, dreams, and desires. Yet, you

# Introduction

also become aware of what holds you back—your wounds and inner obstacles. In the process of working with yourself in this intimate way, you gently develop self-love and self-acceptance.

## *Become empowered and unstoppable*

Here's what I've learned by practicing this work for almost 25 years: I'm unstoppable. I've overcome so many internal obstacles. For example, I had a deep fear of abandonment due to my dad's death as a child. This fear of abandonment was influencing my romantic relationships in the form of fear of intimacy, being afraid to love and lose the partner, and an unwillingness to get close to men. I decided that no matter what it took, I was going to be in a happy, secure, long-term romantic partnership.

I used this process to create that for myself. Did it take a lot of self-work? Yes. Did I have to confront deep inner fears and release them? Yes. Did I have to let go of behaviors and patterns that were keeping me from being in that kind of relationship? Yes. Did it take time? Yes. And was it worth it? Yes. Now, I'm in a very happy, loving, and supportive marriage, and I thank this process for helping me get there.

What I also know about myself now is that if I do the work (and this work is gentle and goes at your pace), I can achieve whatever I want to in life. I am empowered and unstoppable because I have experienced multiple successes in overcoming my challenges. I also know an effective secret to creating whatever I set my mind to. As you create some success with this work, your self-confidence and self-belief will increase and propel you to reach for greater and greater achievements.

According to Ian Robertson, author of *The Winner Effect*, experiencing a win changes your neurochemistry and makes it more likely that you'll experience subsequent wins. Even setting a small goal and achieving it will produce dopamine in the brain and hard-wire you for that experience of success, boosting your confidence. As you experience wins and successes with this Moon practice, you'll become increasingly bold, confident, and self-assured that you can achieve bigger goals and dreams.

## What is Activating Lunar Alchemy?

I consider this work an alchemical process. Symbolically, it's the process of *turning lead into gold*, but not on the literal level of these minerals. Rather, the alchemical process referred to here is the transformation of the human soul. Lead is the metal of Saturn, who is the god of our karma, limitations, suffering, and responsibility. Gold is the metal of the Sun, which signifies our spirit self, the golden self, and our higher conscious awareness. We conduct this alchemical work through the soul self, the silver self, symbolized by the Moon (the metal element being silver). The silver self is one aspect of the container of our soul, which holds all that we have accomplished and experienced in this life and previous lives.

| **Astrological Body** | Saturn | Sun | Moon |
|---|---|---|---|
| **Element** | Lead | Gold | Silver |
| **Key concepts** | Limitations, structure, authority, responsibility, karma, timing | Spirit, Golden self, higher self, potential, | Soul, Silver self, emotions, subconscious self, etheric body |

# Introduction

Doing the work addressed in detail in this book is a process of transmutation. You're transmuting your internal limitations (lead), informed by your childhood programming, life traumas, and karma, into the manifestation of your best life, informed by your spirit and potential self (gold). This transmutation process is accomplished through very practical means of attuning to the Moon's rhythm and working creatively and magically with the self through Moon Wheels.

In psychological terms, you're working in a dynamic process to become conscious of your subconscious and unconscious limitations and change them. You're also working with your higher self and your super consciousness to tap into and develop your dreams, desires and creativity, which generally require you to get out of your comfort zone, grow, and bring forth your potential.

It's important to note here that the way you experience the Moon's rhythm from the Earth is always in relationship to the Sun. The Earth is the perspective from which we view the Moon. The Sun's light is the reflected light we see throughout the Moon cycle. When the Moon is new, it's dark and hidden because it's in alignment with the Sun. In the First Quarter, the Sun and Moon form a 90-degree angle in the sky, illuminating the right half of the Moon as seen on Earth. At the Full Moon, the Moon fully reflects the Sun and illuminates the entire side of the Moon that we see. At the Last Quarter, the Sun and Moon again form a 90-degree angle, illuminating the left half of the Moon.

Consider these aspects symbolically for the alchemical process of the self: the higher self (superconscious) and emotional self (subconscious) come together at the New Moon and come to a consensus about what to create. Then, they're in an active square at the first quarter, waxing moon, encouraging you to take action to support the growth. At the Full Moon, the higher self and emotional self are in dynamic opposition; as the Moon is reflecting the light and conscious awareness of the Sun, it's a time to self-reflect. Finally, as the Moon wanes, it again forms an active square to the Sun, giving you an opportunity to let go of the old and whatever isn't in alignment with what you're attempting to create.

In his book, *The Tarot: A Key to the Wisdom of the Ages*, Paul Foster Case states, "The Moon symbolizes the reflected light of the subconscious."

The cyclical rhythm of the Moon stimulates your soul's rhythm, your energy field, your emotions, and your subconscious. It moves your past experiences in and out of your present awareness. In this practice, you consciously engage with the Moon's rhythm to develop your awareness of the soul self and what's coming to your conscious awareness from your subconscious. You also invite the spirit self to inform you of where you're going and to bring forth your potential, your best life, and your fulfillment.

I have studied and practiced energy healing, the Native American Medicine Wheel, and Egyptian Mysteries with Reverend Rosalyn Bruyere and Ken Weintrub of the Healing Light Center Church (HLCC). I am an ordained minister of the HLCC Crucible Program. For the past 30 years, I have also studied astrology, ancient alchemical texts, and the alchemical Qabalah, which provides esoteric teachings on how to align with the Great Work, the self-conscious work of evolving the self in harmony with God. At its heart, this work is a mystical and magical doctrine for how to change, transform, and heal to live a life of spiritual

# Introduction

abundance. The means, however, are a very practical application of alchemy, magic, and energy healing, which anyone committed to healing and growing can practice.

Overall, this practice has two elements to its structure: the Moon's Cycle and the Moon Wheels. The Moon's Cycle is the rhythm we attune to for gentle change and healing. The Moon Wheels are a ritualistic practice you create at the four main phases of the Moon Cycle.

I deliberately chose to use the word 'magic' in each of the chapter titles. For many years, I struggled with whether this work was magical or not. This work is very practical and could be put in the category of mindset work. However, I have experienced countless miracles, manifestations, and healings as a result of the Moon work, most of which seemed to come to pass in a mysterious way.

One thing I have observed in practicing Lunar Alchemy is that if I continue to take action toward my dreams and desires and do the inner work on myself to make way in my psyche for the manifestation, the Divine meets me more than halfway. It delivers the manifestation (usually better) than what I have asked for.

Dion Fortune, the author of many books on mystical, occult, and magical practice based on the Qabalah says, "Magic is the art of changing consciousness at will."

After 25 years of study on the Moon, the psyche, and the Soul, I understand and concur with Dion Fortune that the human spirit is essentially magical, and you can bring forth what you deeply desire by changing your consciousness. Working with the conscious self, the subconscious self, and the vast potentiality of the superconscious self is central to this magical process.

# Activating Lunar Alchemy

For the sake of the chapter titles, the term *magic* refers to the distinct modes and qualities of how you apply your energy and awareness. For example, your *dreams*, which are the soft, nebulous, and expansive callings of your spirit, are distinctly different in form and quality than your *attention*, which is a sharp and narrow way to focus your mental energy working with your executive functions (or third eye).

When I first started this work over 20 years ago, I was attempting to manifest my best life. I learned about 'seeding the Moon' from Jan Spiller's book, *New Moon Astrology*. I had a few successes early on, but I remained struggling and unfulfilled in my life. In the practice of seeding the Moon, you only work with the Moon at the New Moon.

I wondered, however, what would happen if I worked with my dreams, goals, and desires like you would in gardening with the Moon. For example, you seed on certain days of the Moon cycle, fertilize on other days, and prune and weed at different aspects of the cycle. This led me to develop this four-step process of working with the Moon cycle.

I hope you enjoy the process of *Activating Lunar Alchemy* as much as I do. Please consider making a commitment to yourself to practice this Moon work for a minimum of three months so you can experience its positive effects in your life. This work takes inner work. It's not a one-and-done activity but rather an ongoing process of developing the self. Like exercising, regularly aligning with the Moon's rhythm is a lifestyle habit.

To start attuning to the Moon now, download your free *Quick Start Key* at https://thesydneyfrancis.com/products/key

# CHAPTER 1

# The Magic of Pain

*"Grief can be the garden of compassion. If you keep your heart open through everything, your pain can become your greatest ally in your life's search for love and wisdom."* – Rumi

*"There is no coming to consciousness without pain."*
*– Carl Jung*

Pain is twice as likely to motivate people to take action than pleasure! I learned that from well-known entrepreneur and investor Dean Graziosi at a marketing seminar and was very surprised. I figured that pleasure would be a bigger motivator, but then I looked at my own life and realized that most of my major decisions and actions were motivated by getting out of pain.

Although I don't want to be in pain, I owe a lot to the pain and suffering in my life, as it has brought me many blessings, growth, and spiritual abundance. I am grateful for pain's teachings and its magic.

It may be hard to believe, but the following are some of the benefits of embracing your pain:

- pain brings you to consciousness
- pain moves you to action
- pain is an ally that shows you the direction of your growth, pleasure, and desires
- pain can give you your greatest gifts and blessings
- pain can be transformed into spiritual abundance

### *Pain brings you to consciousness*
My story of growth and the story behind *Activating Lunar Alchemy* has been about getting out of emotional pain. My dad died of brain cancer when I was 10. The grief, loss, and feelings of abandonment cast a shadow over much of my life.

After my dad's memorial service, my mom told me to move on, look forward, and not dwell in the past. In hindsight, I know she meant well and gave me her best advice, but my loss and grief were deep. I missed my dad, and I didn't know how to process his death. When I expressed sadness, pain, or grief, I got in trouble. I took to hiding my grief and internalized it in order to cope.

I was 18, at college, and taking Adolescent Development, when my grief resurfaced. I was overwhelmed with a despairing chasm

# The Magic of Pain

of sadness for several weeks. This is when my grieving process began.

I graduated from college at 20 and decided to reject a 'real' job in Connecticut so that I could work with kids at a summer camp. I felt that my direction was in psychology and working with people. I ended up getting a job in the kitchen, which was not as kid oriented as I had hoped.

The kitchen manager was a married, 45-year-old man who did long-term kitchen and catering gigs. Initially, we formed a friendship. I was a hard worker and became his reliable assistant in the kitchen. However, as the summer wore on, he expressed interest in dating me. I told him I was only interested in a professional and collegial relationship.

We worked long days together, starting at 5 am to prepare breakfast and ending at 8 pm after the kitchen was cleaned up and reorganized. As the summer wore on, I became more and more valuable as the kitchen assistant, and I was promoted to manager in the second kitchen, serving the older kids.

The kitchen manager and I went out to celebrate my promotion. After we finished our meal, he reached over and kissed me. *I lost it.* I had been honest and clear multiple times that I wasn't interested. I felt so frustrated and discouraged that I couldn't make myself clear. I had been date raped two times previously and had experienced a lot of sexual harassment and similar negative sexual encounters. I felt powerless and frustrated. I was angry at him, although I was enraged at myself for being in this situation.

## Activating Lunar Alchemy

I returned to my room at the camp, packed up my stuff, and then drove off in a frantic hurry. I had a couple of days off at that time, so I headed to Mesa Verde National Park.

I drove over the mountain pass between Aspen and Granite, Colorado. I had a quick lunch in Aspen and got back in the car. I continued to drive toward Mesa Verde.

At one point, I looked down to change the radio station, and suddenly, I was swerving out of control. I accidentally pressed the accelerator instead of the brake. I swerved left into the other lane and then did a hard right. Then, I drove off a cliff into the Colorado River. I had a moment where I thought I was going to die. My life literally flashed before my eyes. Then I crashed into the bottom of the riverbed.

After climbing up the riverbank, some men in a passing blue truck picked me up and said they knew a reliable Honda mechanic in a nearby town. The mechanic also had a tow truck.

Hours later, my car was towed to the shop. I found a motel and some food and went to bed. Miraculously, the next morning, my car was ready for me to drive away. The mechanic stayed at the repair shop late into the night to fix my wheel wells and tires and do the repairs.

A few things, like the frame of the car, were permanently damaged, but I drove away. I headed back toward the accident sight. As I neared it, I burst into tears. I pulled over and began sobbing uncontrollably.

# The Magic of Pain

I was coming out of shock from the accident. I was also coming out of shock from the incident I had with the kitchen manager the previous day.

At some point, I felt so powerless and alone that I prayed for help. I felt that my life was careening helplessly out of control and had been for some time. A presence came to me, like a light being or an angel. She conveyed to me that everything would be okay and that I could heal and change.

A family friend had given me Louise Hay's book *You Can Heal Your Life* as a graduation gift. I was guided by this angel to start with reading and doing the practices in this book. Although it took a terrifying car accident, this pain brought me to consciousness.

## *Pain moves you to action*

I wanted to get out of the pain that had led up to the moment of the accident. In hindsight, I had been out of my body since the kiss. I was in a type of emotional trance when I drove away from the summer camp. I was dissociated.

The accident and the angelic visit brought me back to myself, and now I wanted to start moving toward healing. I read *You Can Heal Your Life* like a textbook. I would read a chapter each week, study it, and practice the exercises daily. I went through a profound period of self-care and healing at this time. Once I was aware of the pain, it moved me to take action.

## *Pain is an ally that shows you the direction of your growth, pleasure, and desires*

Over the course of the next few months, as I read Louise Hay religiously, I began to question what I wanted out of life. What was my purpose? What would give me meaning and fulfillment in work?

I didn't return to the summer camp, but rather, after a period of solitude in Moab, Utah, where I hiked at the national parks, explored the canyons, and swam in the Colorado River, I ended up moving to Seattle.

I needed a job. I wanted to do meaningful work. I really didn't know what that meant to me. After thinking I wanted to be an engineer, I ended up studying visual art and psychology in college. Graduating at 20 with no obvious work skills, I felt lost and adrift.

Again, I went back to praying and asking for help. I was having a hard time finding a job and had no direction. I was experiencing the lows of post-graduate depression.

It was October 1993; I took a nap one afternoon and dreamt I was at a grocery store. I was looking through the aisles. There were a lot of familiar and beautiful items. For example, there were those old Coca-Cola cans with Santa in vivid blues and reds, yet they were rusty. That wasn't what I was looking for.

I kept going up and down the aisles, and then something called to me. I followed this sound, song, or calling to the end of an aisle. In front of me were glass jars filled with beautiful pink, violet, blue, and iridescent jellybeans. They were sparkling, glowing, and radiating. This heavenly iridescent light told me that my work and purpose were in spiritual healing work.

I woke up from this nap feeling so happy, relieved, and enthusiastic. I had direction, inspiration, and clarity. Within weeks, I went

## The Magic of Pain

to a live seminar with Deepak Chopra. Then, I enrolled in an introductory workshop at Barbara Brennan's Hands of Light school on Long Island. I also found a job tutoring a boy with ADHD who had suffered early childhood trauma and sexual abuse.

### *Pain can give you your greatest gifts and blessings*

Although I don't want to experience pain and suffering, pain has taught me so much, and I'm grateful for it. Having grieved for my dad for many years, I gained a lot of compassion for others experiencing grief and loss. Physical and emotional pain protects us from dangerous or damaging stimuli. Pain is an indicator to pay attention to something happening within you. Pain gives you invaluable information if you lean into it, listen to it, and give it the attention it requests.

For so long, I was running away from and pushing my pain deep down. I didn't want to feel, address, or work with it. That was one of the benefits of the car accident; I finally had to stop, feel, and confront the pain I was in. When I surrendered to it, I went through one of the most profound healing periods of my life. Much of what I've learned and developed, especially as it applies to the practices in this book, has been developed in relation to getting out of pain into comfort, ease, and pleasure.

### *Pain can be transformed into spiritual abundance*

I've developed more sensitivity to my body, mind, emotions, and spirit over the years of studying healing, psychology, and spirituality. I've found, in particular, when it comes to emotional pain, that working with my pain moves me toward spiritual growth and abundance.

In doing this Moon work, you actively pursue your dreams and goals. What generally comes up at some point in the process is you'll have to face some sort of resistance, block, or pain. The pain is often a fear, although there are many other types of emotional pain, such as shame, doubt, grief, or regret. As you work with and address what this pain is telling you, you begin to release it, heal it, learn from it, and grow from it. This transformational process leads to your spiritual abundance, encompassing your physical, mental, emotional, and spiritual well-being.

## What is pain?

Although pain feels real enough, the definition is somewhat philosophical. The International Association for the Study of Pain's definition is the following:

An unpleasant sensory and emotional experience associated with, or resembling that associated with actual or potential tissue damage, and is expanded upon by the addition of six keynotes and the etymology of the word pain for further valuable context:

- Pain is always a personal experience that is influenced to varying degrees by biological, psychological, and social factors.
- Pain and nociception are different phenomena. Pain cannot be inferred solely from activity in sensory neurons.
- Through their life experiences, individuals learn the concept of pain.
- A person's report of an experience of pain should be respected.
- Although pain usually serves an adaptive role, it may have adverse effects on function and social and psychological well-being.

## The Magic of Pain

- Verbal description is only one of several behaviors to express pain; the inability to communicate doesn't negate the possibility that a human or a nonhuman animal experiences pain.

The above definition is scientific and medically oriented and is limited to pain caused by tissue damage. According to Western science, there is no such thing as psychological pain. Western science describes emotional pain in terms of suffering, anguish, and distress.

There is no definitive or official definition of psychological pain. In my experience, however, psychological (defined as mental or emotional) pain can be much more painful than physical pain and more unbearable. I read several articles that say suicides are initiated from psychological pain more often than from physical pain.

Emotional pain is anguishing and causes suffering. For the sake of this book, I am going to call 'psychological anguish' *emotional pain*. Throughout your life, you experience a variety of sensory, emotional experiences that register as emotional pain, such as fear, anger, resentment, sadness, depression, hopelessness, shame, humiliation, worthlessness, anxiety, terror, helplessness, guilt, powerlessness, overwhelm, doubt, and worry. These are a sampling of painful feelings and emotions. Emotional pain can be very debilitating.

I have suffered from anxiety and depression throughout my life and have experienced suicidal depression a few times. It was not caused by physical suffering but rather emotional pain. About six months after my first daughter Sophia was born, I gave up my job to move to another town with Sophia's dad so he could get a better-paying job. This was the first time in my life that I had not worked. I enjoyed staying home with Sophia, but the isolation and not working at a regular job were unbearable to me. After several months of this, I was in a deep depression. I remember lying in bed, wishing and wondering if there was a way I could die. This suicidal depression lasted several weeks. Then, I broke out of it and realized I needed to return to my previous home and get a job.

I don't make light of that fact. Depression of any kind and suicidal depression are deeply painful and almost insufferable. Please seek immediate professional help if you are experiencing that. I share that story to relate to and empathize with the emotional pain you may experience. Your emotional pain is real. Pay attention to it. The pain is attempting to tell you something or get you to take action to get out of pain.

As an ordained minister, I am also very concerned with the concept of spiritual pain. Also called 'existential pain,' spiritual pain can be defined as a 'self-identified experience of personal discomfort, or actual or potential harm, triggered by a threat to a person's relationship with God or a higher power.'

Spiritual pain has been described and defined in the following ways:

- A desolate sense of meaninglessness
- Loss of a sense of self
- Feelings of annihilation and impending separation
- The pain and suffering of life itself
- Soul pain
- Despair
- The disconnection or abandonment by God

## The Magic of Pain

- Living without a sense of faith in a higher power
- The inability to relate to a higher power or the sacred

Spiritual pain is important to include in this book because the spiritual process described here aims at developing our sense of self, meaning, well-being, and connection with a higher power, even if that higher power is conceived as one's spirit self. Living a life full of meaning, purpose, spiritual well-being, and a healthy sense of self is *spiritual abundance*.

The tagline of this book is 'The Mystical Art of Transmuting Emotional Pain into Spiritual Abundance.' Emotional and spiritual pain are at the heart of the matter discussed in this book because, in my experience, psychological pain, existential pain, and soul suffering are what you ultimately struggle with in order to create a better life for yourself.

## How do you get out of pain and into comfort or pleasure?

In this book, I will describe the process and the method for transmuting your pain into spiritual abundance. In essence, the steps are the following: you define what you want, including your dreams, goals, and desires. Keeping in mind what you want, you begin to take supportive action toward making those dreams, desires, and goals a reality. Then, you observe what's happening in your life, including how you feel, what's going on, and what's real for you. Finally, you ritualistically release the pain, limitations, or behaviors that are holding you back. This process helps you listen to, identify, and recognize the pain you're experiencing, usually on a subconscious level, and transmute it into a source of strength or a gift that propels you in the direction of your fulfillment.

## Activating Lunar Alchemy

Bringing your dreams to reality and living your best life is possible if you're willing to do the work. In this book, you will learn an easy-to-follow, four-step process to move toward your dreams and remove the obstacles. A life full of meaningful work, improved health, happy and supportive relationships, and spiritual purpose is well worth the effort.

### ACTIONS YOU CAN TAKE AS A RESULT OF READING THIS CHAPTER:

1. Consider the story of your pain.

2. Explore the connection between your pain and your desires/purpose/contribution.

3. Connect to the pain to start the healing process.

# CHAPTER 2

# The Magic of the Moon

*"Energy can't be created or destroyed, and energy flows. It must be in a direction, with some kind of internal, emotive, spiritual direction. It must have some effect somewhere."*
– Keanu Reeves

*"The Moon has been up there as long as evolution has been taking place, and lunar rhythms are embedded in the life cycles of many organisms."* – Dr. Tom White

## Why the Moon?

When I see the Moon, I am frequently struck by wonder, awe, and a sense of beauty. It's always there, constant, yet changing. The Moon brings a sense of psychical comfort and familiarity as it silently witnesses life on Earth.

The Moon is magical, and the more I learn about its history, science, and geology, as well as its symbolic meaning in astrology and the occult doctrines, the more I feel love, enthusiasm, and inspiration about the Moon. The work of *Activating Lunar Alchemy* is a spiritual practice of attuning to the Moon's rhythm, designed to gently promote spiritual growth and healing.

There are many benefits to working with the magic of the Moon, such as:

- Attuning to the Moon's rhythm promotes healing and self-regulation
- Working with the timing of the Moon teaches you to work smarter, not harder
- The Moon stimulates life, growth, creation, and regeneration
- The Moon's rhythm teaches a pattern for transmutation, allowing you to transform painful patterns into strength, resilience, and blessings
- Utilizing the Moon as a mirror increases your self-love and self-acceptance
- Engaging in this consistent Moon practice develops your intuition and awareness

You're a part of the Earth's electromagnetic field, and you're influenced by the rhythmical movement of the Moon. As far as the Moon cycle is concerned, you're like a fish in water. It's hard to consciously be aware of something that's so much a part of the fabric of your being and the environment in which you grow up. However, the Moon does move you, your energy, and your psyche, like the tides of the ocean. Consciously attuning to the Moon's rhythm is empowering and regenerative.

## *Attuning to the Moon's rhythm promotes healing and self-regulation*

Did you know that the Moon steadies the Earth's wobble, regulates its spin, and stabilizes its seasons? Without the Moon, the Earth would be spinning frenetically fast as it orbits around the Sun. Without the Moon, the Earth would experience radical shifts in the tilt of its axis, causing temperature extremes that would be unsustainable for life. The Moon provides the Earth with a steadying influence and a rhythmical balance that supports growth, life, and gentle change.

In this process, you're proactively attuning your energy and actions to the Moon's gentle rhythm. At first, it may seem mechanical, but I've discovered that this process helps you reveal the *circalunar* rhythm that already underlies your life. By increasing your awareness of this rhythm and working with it, you can experience profound healing.

Rhythm is important for healing, balance, and self-regulation. Like inhaling and exhaling, inward and outward, yin and yang, the waxing and waning of the Moon brings alternating benefits to you, promoting wholeness, order, and balance in your body, mind, emotions, and spirit.

## *Working with the timing of the Moon teaches you to work smarter, not harder*

One of the reasons I started to work on attuning to the Moon cycle was to optimize my synchronicity with divine timing based on astrological cycles. As part of my interest in the Moon, I also studied and practiced gardening with the Moon cycle. In gardening with the Moon, you optimize the energies of the Earth, Nature, Sun and the Moon by working with the Moon's rhythm to guide planting, fertilizing, harvesting, and pruning times. Gardening with the Moon brings more life vitality to your plants, your garden, and your soil and encourages greater growth and productivity in the garden.

I believe your soul and psyche can be cultivated like a garden. You have both a circadian rhythm, connected to night and day, and a circalunar rhythm, connected to the Moon cycle. Working with the Moon's rhythm to create a project or bring forth a dream makes the process easier because you're working with the cycles and the movement of the energy. Applying the Moon's rhythm to your life allows you to work with the energy and have better results.

## *The Moon stimulates life, growth, creation, and regeneration*

The Sun, Moon, and Earth are in an optimal relationship to give rise to life. You've probably heard that Earth resides in the 'Goldilocks Zone' of the solar system, a place that has just the right conditions for life. The relationship between the Earth and the Moon and its synergistic orbit also supports the conditions that give rise to life. The Moon regulates the tides and gives movement and agitation to the oceans, providing the ideal environment for the first life on Earth to catalyze. Not only did simple life form from the oceans, but it continued to form, change and evolve. Scientists believe this evolutionary growth

# The Magic of the Moon

is due to the consistency of the Moon's rhythm, its effect on the tides, and its stabilizing force on the climate.[1]

In addition, the reproductive cycles of many animals are related to the Moon cycle, supporting the continuation and propagation of life.[2] Literally and symbolically, the Moon continues to support growth, life, and evolution on Earth. In this Moon work, you tap into the creative and generative aspects of the Moon.

### *The Moon rhythm teaches a pattern for transmutation, allowing you to transform painful patterns into strength, resilience, and abundance*

Lunar Alchemy teaches you a method for aligning with the Moon's rhythm to induce an alchemical process—transmutation. Transmutation is the process of changing "some essential element into a superior form."[3]

Consider that the evolutionary growth and regeneration I speak about above are related to this idea of transmutation, changing from one elemental form to a superior elemental form. Is that not what happens when you grow and evolve? You become a superior version of yourself and are no longer the original version.

As you aspire to grow and deliberately create your life, you're being pulled toward this superior self, your greater potential, and you're inviting change. In order to support new growth, you have to let go of the old or transmute it into an energy that sustains the new state. In this Moon work, the old and unsupportive environment generally consists of behaviors, habits, addictions, damaging emotions, limiting beliefs, and the like. For example, it took me many years of transmuting my fear of failure, perfectionism, and self-doubt to actively start writing this book. I would start and stop, writing many iterations over the last two years. Moon cycle after Moon cycle, I transmuted the fear into courage and faith in myself and my work, taking baby steps forward to make this book a reality.

For the sake of this book, I am referring to transmutation as a psychological and energetic process. The energetic process of transmutation in this work happens at the level of the psyche and the aura, also known as the human electromagnetic field. As you work on becoming aware of your painful and damaging patterns and transmuting them, you become lighter and calibrate your energy to create the right environment and bring forth what you desire.

### *Utilizing the Moon as a mirror increases your self-love and self-acceptance*

This is a self-reflective process. You supply the dreams, the action, the reflection, and the letting go in order to move forward and bring forth your best life. The by-products of this self-oriented healing process are self-love and self-acceptance. As you create more in your life, you naturally come up against beliefs that you hold about yourself, old childhood narratives, and painful patterns you carry as a result of your life experiences. This Moon cycle process invites you to embrace these patterns and stories, let go of the pain, and develop self-love and self-acceptance in their place.

### *Engaging in this consistent Moon practice develops your intuition and awareness*

As you increase your self-conscious awareness through this Moon work, you also develop your sensitivity, sense of self, and intuition. When you're not cognitively aware of what's happening within you—what you're sensing and feeling—it's difficult to access the information from your intuition. In essence, you're not listening to or paying attention to the signals. As you tune into yourself and your creative rhythm through the Moon work, you rekindle that awareness and your ability to hear, sense, and feel what your intuition is communicating to you.

## What is the Magic of the Moon?

According to contemporary scientific evidence, the miraculous synergy of the Earth and Moon is due to its cataclysmic beginnings. In the formative epoch of the solar system, the Earth and Moon were born from the same original planetary body. There was an earlier version of Earth that was split into pieces by a collision with another celestial planetoid, Theia. This calamity formed the Earth and Moon you know today. The dating of radioactive isotopes from Moon rock demonstrates that the Earth and the Moon were formed from the same substances at the same time,[4] like geological fraternal twins.

Scientists now believe the Earth and Moon formed together in a swirling donut of molten metal called a *synestia*.[5] This synestia supported the reformation of the Earth and the seed growth of the Moon. As the synestia cooled and condensed, the Earth and its Moon formed in a pair.

Why is this magical? Like in human life, it's hard to know yourself without being in a relationship with another. Self-conscious awareness begins in early childhood during the Mirror Stage when children begin to recognize themselves in the mirror. This can spark an identity crisis as the child realizes they're separate from their caregiver, but it's also an opportunity for individuation and psychological development. The Moon is a mirror for the Earth, and symbolically, you can use it as a mirror for your continued individuation, development, and growth.

I used to think that the Moon orbited the Earth, as is the common understanding of the Moon. However, the Earth and Moon are in a mutual orbiting pattern, moving together and influencing one another. They affect one another. The Moon creates a tidal motion that slows the Earth down, and the tidal motion pushes the Moon further away from Earth.

The Moon is a fascinating companion. The Earth is in a constant relationship with the Moon, and this synergistic relationship has given rise to incredible miracles, such as life on this planet, the tides, and the conditions for evolution.

This Moon work is a mystical and esoteric process of attuning to the Moon's rhythm. Modern science is just beginning to discover the ways in which the Earth, plants, and animals are connected and related to the Moon. Recent research on sea louse shows that they have both a circadian rhythm to determine if it's night or day and a circatidal rhythm synchronized with the tides to help them navigate the water for their feeding and survival.[6]

Spiritual traditions throughout the ages and from all over the world have honored and worked with the magic and rhythm of the Moon. A good example of this is Easter Sunday. Easter Sunday changes each year because it's a lunisolar holiday; it's on the Sunday after the first Full Moon following the Spring Equinox. This is how Lent, Mardi Gras, and the Catholic holidays connected to Easter are assigned in the modern calendar. Unfortunately, in modern American culture, these ways, traditions, and sacred mysteries regarding the Moon have been largely lost, shamed, or obscured. But many cultures and

# The Magic of the Moon

spiritual traditions, such as Judaism, Hinduism, and Chinese culture, still celebrate lunisolar holidays.

My interest in the Moon deepened as I began to study astrology and was introduced to the book *New Moon Astrology* by Jan Spiller. In this book, Spiller writes about the power of the New Moon and the astrological timing for 'seeding' your wishes to bring them to fruition.

I started my practice of 'seeding the Moon' around 2001. This practice inspired many questions in me. I was aware that Moon calendars and farmer's almanacs provided lunar guidance on the optimal timing used in gardening, fishing, pruning, cutting your hair, and so forth. So, I wondered if there was also optimal timing to cultivate your wishes in the rest of the Moon cycle after 'seeding' the Moon. Could I coordinate my activities with the Moon to ensure a successful outcome?

I began to investigate and practice gardening with the Moon alongside my astrological studies. I observed the Moon cycle daily and recorded a little sketch of the Moon in my journal. The Moon cycle is very patterned; you see the thin waxing crescent each month in almost the same position in the western sky before it sets; the first quarter or waxing half-moon is above your head at sunset; the Full Moon rises in the East just after sunset; and the last quarter or waning half-moon is above your head at sunrise.

Later, I began to track the Moon through the astrological signs of the zodiac and throughout the calendar year. For example, today, the Sun is in Aquarius, and the Moon is in Scorpio. It will form its last quarter tomorrow. I record this daily in my journal next to the calendar date (with my little sketch of the Moon).

## Activating Lunar Alchemy

There's a lot to learn from observing the Moon's rhythm and studying its patterns. This is especially helpful if you garden with the Moon because where the New Moons fall in terms of the solar calendar and the seasons is very important for figuring out the planting cycle and when the first and last frosts will be.

Last year (2023), the New Moons came in the early degrees of the zodiac signs, so I began planting in February. This year, the New Moons are near the ending degrees of the zodiac signs, so I will likely plant later in the year. This affects the entire growing season, as it tells you when the harvest will come to fruition and when you need to put your garden to bed before the freezing nights of autumn.

Over 20 years of inquiry, practice, and application of working with the Moon's rhythm has yielded a lot of success and insight into the magic of the Moon. There's still more to learn and be discovered in the practical application of these concepts.

## The Healing Power of Rhythm

> *"The Qabalah teaches a wiser doctrine...It recognizes that rhythm is the basis of life, not steady forward progress."* - Dion Fortune, The Mystical Qabalah

The Moon waxes and wanes from our point of view from Earth. The Moon also helps stabilize the Earth's rotational tilt on its axis, allowing the rhythmical patterns of the seasons and a regulatory effect on the Earth's temperatures and climate. Rhythm underlies all of life! You have a heartbeat. You inhale and exhale. You have a circadian rhythm that influences your sleep and wake cycles. Your hormones have a rhythm, such as

# The Magic of the Moon

the production of cortisol, which gets you up in the morning and the production of melatonin, which allows you to rest and get to sleep at night. You also have a reproductive rhythm, which is especially obvious in women's monthly *moon* cycle. Chronobiologists have gathered evidence that the Moon affects your monthly sleep cycle, resulting in less sleep at the full Moon and more sleep at the new Moon.[7]

## Moon's Rhythm

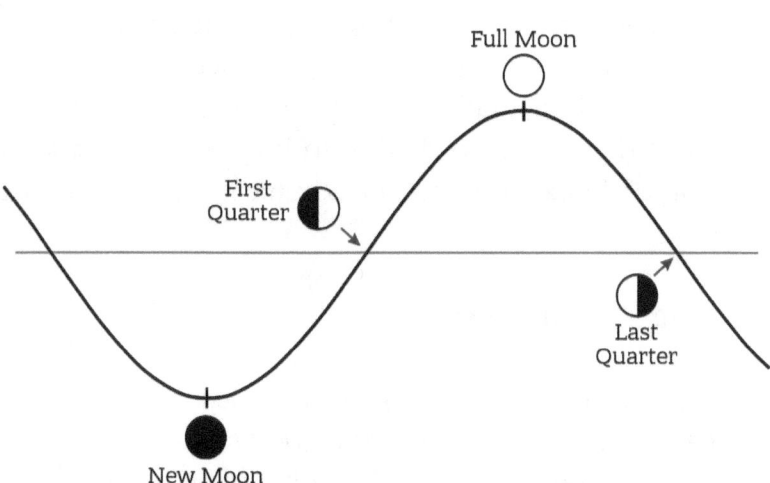

A regular rhythm, such as the Moon cycle, is healing because it's 'whole,' which is the root word of healing. If you just inhaled without the ability to exhale, what would happen? Balance and movement are needed to keep a healthy rhythm. One thing I have seen in attuning to the Moon's rhythm is that striving for a sense of balance between the input and output of life is critically important. For much of my life, I was extremely out of balance in my daily, weekly, monthly, and annual rhythm. I worked too hard, didn't get enough rest, and put others' needs first until I broke down into a nervous wreck. My adrenals literally crashed in 2017 while I was working at a demanding elementary school teaching job.

Our American culture tells us to go, go, go, work, work, work, progress, progress, progress, without honoring the need for and balancing effects of rest, relaxation, and ingress of the Spirit. The Moon does things differently, at least from Earth's point of view. The Moon starts out dark, quiet, resting and inward. Then, it waxes and gently builds up the energy. At the peak of its building energy, it gets full, outward, and illuminated. Serenely, the Moon wanes, taking down the energy and returning inwards. This is a circular, healing rhythm—a balance of outward and inward, of build-up and break down, of output and input. In contrast, if there were no rhythm to life, life would cease to exist, as it would stagnate, have no movement, and become inert.

## The Magic of Timing

> *"Your best work involves timing. If someone wrote the best hip hop song of all time in the Middle Ages, he had bad timing."* - Scott Adams

Another of the Moon's magical aspects is timing. Timing is a concept related to rhythm, but there's a distinct difference. Timing is about optimizing your energy and efforts in synchronicity with the cycles. For example, the Moon moves and regulates the tides, and the ocean waves you experience at the beach. Imagine that you want to body surf and ride a wave. The timing of your actions and efforts makes all the difference. To catch the wave, you need to start swimming as it approaches to catch its momentum and ride it effortlessly to shore. If your timing is off, you miss it. The wave does the work for you. Consider

## The Magic of the Moon

the resistance of swimming in the ocean against the surf. It's a struggle as you push against the water and the current.

With Lunar Alchemy, you're working with the timing and the energetic waves of the Moon, letting the waxing and waning power move you forward. When you harmonize your efforts with the Moon, life gets easier and becomes less of a struggle to 'make it happen,' like riding the wave. Living life without respect for timing can be a struggle, much like swimming against the tide.

Gardening with the Moon is also about timing. Do you plant your seeds in winter when the ground is hard and frozen, hoping they'll come up and prosper? Or do you plant in spring when the ground is soft and warm, and the momentum of the season is building to summer? In gardening, you're optimizing the timing of the building energy and the hidden cycles of nature's processes.

Timing is a feature of the etheric energy field, also known as the etheric matrix or etheric template. The etheric matrix is like the blueprint of intelligence that underlies the material, the Universe. Everything has an underlying intelligence structure, composed and organized on the etheric template. The etheric matrix is like DNA, which provides the underlying information, organization, and structure for organic life.

In *The Mystical Qabalah*, Dion Fortune says that the Moon, affiliated with the Holy Sephiroth of Yesod, is the 'ether of the wise' and that you can mold this etheric energy, which she calls *ectoplasm*, with your thoughts.

You mold the etheric energy with your thoughts when you 'seed the Moon' with your dreams, desires, and goals while making your New Moon wheel. You reinforce the molding of the etheric energy by taking action toward your dreams. At the Full Moon, you're 'reading' the etheric energy via self-reflection by observing what's happening in your life. In essence, you're observing the discrepancy between your ideal situation (etheric) and what's real and material in your life. In the Last Quarter, you tap into the etheric energy again to let go of what isn't working and reinforce the dream situation or ideal outcome, transforming the energy.

This process of molding the etheric energy with your thoughts can be greatly enhanced by visualization, which I talk about more in 'The Magic of Dreaming.' As an artist, I create an art piece in my imagination before I create its three-dimensional form. I think about what I want and create it in my thoughts, sometimes spending days, weeks, or months working on visualizing a piece. When it's clear in my mind's eye, I take action through planning, sketching, and creative processes to bring that idea into the material realm.

## The Moon as a Mirror

> *"The Moon says nothing for itself, but it says plenty about us. We project our dreams and our fervor onto its mottled surface, and it serves as a mirror, both figuratively and literally. It reflects sunlight and even the Earth's own light, ashen earthshine, back to us."*
> *- Rebecca Boyle, Our Moon*

The Moon is a mirror on many levels, available for you to utilize. The Moon reflects the light of the Earth, more clearly seen in the Moon's waxing and waning crescent phases. It also reflects

## The Magic of the Moon

the light of the Sun to us. Symbolically, the Moon reflects your subconscious back to you so you can see and work with it.

In this Moon work, you use this mirroring and reflective quality of the Moon to enhance your cognitive awareness of invisible subconscious patterns and programs. For example, in the previous section, I talked about using the Moon to observe the discrepancy between your dream ideal and your results. By looking at your results (via the Full Moon) in your health, work, income, relationships, and spiritual life, you can begin to see the subconscious patterns that are running the show.

One of the most profound examples of this happened when I was dating after my divorce. I would date a man for a few weeks to a few months. The relationship would follow a similar pattern and then end. The men would say they weren't into long-term relationships; they didn't want to commit; they appeared to be averse to emotional intimacy.

For quite a while, I blamed these guys for the fact that I was unable to have a lasting relationship. Then, one Full Moon, in doing this self-reflective work, I realized it wasn't them. IT WAS ME! I had a deep fear of emotional intimacy. On the surface, I longed for closeness and the depth of emotional connection. But underneath the surface, subconsciously, I was pushing them away. I was choosing men to date who weren't able to give me what I was seeking.

As a result of the Moon work, this insight was a real breakthrough for me and my ability to get into a long-term, emotionally intimate relationship. I began to explore and release my fears of emotional intimacy. I worked on reparenting my scared, abandoned inner child, who was deeply afraid of losing love. I worked on my attachment style as an 'anxious attached' person until I was energetically, mentally, and emotionally ready to be in a secure, loving, intimate, and long-term relationship. Much of the work I did to make this dramatic change in my life was inner work. In my opinion, this is one of the profound magical prospects of working with the Moon as a mirror.

All the work you do with Lunar Alchemy is a process of working with yourself. You work with your conscious self, subconscious self, and super-conscious self to deliberately create the life of your dreams. Working with the Moon as a mirror helps you see what remains hidden from your self-awareness and change what's keeping you from your best life.

## The Moon's Creative Magic

> *"It's possible you've heard of circadian rhythms. They refer to day and night cycles driven by Earth orbiting the Sun. Human circadian rhythms are easily thrown off by jet lag or a change of the clocks. But there are also circalunar rhythms, which are tied to lunar cycles."*
> *- Kerry Lotzof*

The Moon cycle is also affiliated with reproduction, generation, conception, and fertility. Many animals have reproductive behaviors that are in sync with the Moon cycle. For example, the bristle worm spawns at the same lunar time each Moon cycle.[8] Most women have their monthly 'moon' in periodicity with the Moon cycle, approximately 28 to 30 days. Moon goddesses, such as Ixchel, a Mayan Moon goddess, are often worshipped for their influence on human fertility and the fertility of the Earth. In gardening with the Moon, there's a connection between 'seeding'

# The Magic of the Moon

on or near the New Moon—a type of conception—and capturing the upbuilding energy of the waxing Moon. Part of the magic of this method is in aligning with the fertile and creative cycle of the Moon to easily bring forth your dreams and desires.

## How do you attune to the magic of the Moon?

In this practice, you attune your energy and actions to the four main phases of the Moon cycle: New Moon, First Quarter, Full Moon, and Last Quarter. This four-part process is for practicality in modern life. You're busy. Making time to do a Moon Wheel approximately once a week is enough to keep you attuned to the Moon's rhythm.

### Moon Cycle

*Reflect* — Full Moon

*Act* — First Quarter

*Listen* — New Moon

*Release* — Last Quarter

Waxing: Increasing, Upbuilding

Waning: Decreasing, Downbuilding

## Activating Lunar Alchemy

At the New Moon, the Sun, Moon and Earth are in alignment. The Moon is between the Sun and Earth and appears invisible. In astrological terms, the Sun and Moon form a 'conjunction.' This is the time for inner work and tapping into your higher self or superconscious self to seed the Moon with your dreams, desires, visions, and goals. Like in a garden, this is the time to 'seed.'

In the first quarter, the Moon makes a 'square' relationship with the Sun and Earth, forming a 90-degree angle in the sky. In astrology, a square aspect is an active aspect. In addition, the Moon is waxing and growing, so this is the time to take supportive action to achieve your dreams, such as watering or fertilizing your garden.

At the Full Moon, the Sun, Moon, and Earth align again. This time, the Moon is on one side of Earth, and the Sun is on the other. This is called an 'opposition' in astrology. If you're sensitive to it, you can feel the heightened energy and tension at the Full Moon. To attune to it, you use the mirroring magic of the moon and the light of spiritual illumination (Sun) to see what's really going on underneath the surface of your awareness.

After the Full Moon, the Moon wanes for about one week to the Last Quarter or waning half-moon. At this time, you have had the insights and time to reflect on what's happening in your life and what needs to be released, cut away, or let go. This is like pruning or weeding the garden to support the growth that you're deliberately and conscientiously cultivating. This is done in concert with the waning energy of the Moon to harmonize with its shedding and dissolving energy.

To attune your energy, actions, and insights with the Moon, you create a series of four distinct Moon Wheels. A Moon Wheel is based on the Native American Medicine Wheel. Making a Moon Wheel is a ritualistic and magical process. At the New Moon, your wheel will be created like a dream map or a vision board. During the First Quarter, your Moon Wheel is more like an action plan or to-do list. At the Full Moon, your wheel is a container for your insights and self-reflection, like a symbolic self-portrait. At the Last Quarter, your Moon Wheel is a ritual platform for letting go, releasing, shedding, and transmuting your old, outmoded energetic patterns.

> **ACTIONS YOU CAN TAKE AS A RESULT OF READING THIS CHAPTER:**
>
> 1. Observe the Moon throughout its cycle and track it in your journal.
>
> 2. Get a copy of a Moon calendar.

# CHAPTER 3

# The Magic of Dreaming

*"When you have a dream that you can't let go of, trust your instincts and pursue it. But remember: Real dreams take work; they take patience, and sometimes they require you to dig down very deep. Be sure you're willing to do that."* – Harvey Mackay

*"Never give up on what you really want to do. The person with big dreams is more powerful than the one with all the facts."* – Albert Einstein

# Activating Lunar Alchemy

*"Reach high, for stars lie hidden in your soul. Dream deep, for every dream precedes the goal."*
*– Pamela Vaull Starr*

The concept of having a dream, meaning a life's ambition or aspiration, wasn't part of the popular vernacular until 1931. The concept of a dream, which means an ideal, like a 'dream girl,' only dates back to around 1850.[9] Although this concept of pursuing your big dream and having the freedom to reach your aspirations is relatively new to human consciousness, it's very important if you want to live a life of meaning and fulfillment.

Having a dream and following it may seem impractical to you at first. However, your dreams come from an innocent, essential, and authentic part of you. They orient you toward your best life and even to some mysterious yet fortuitous outcomes.

There are many benefits of following your dreams, including:

- Dreams give you a sense of purpose and fulfillment
- Dreams stay with you
- Dreams provide orientation and direction
- Dreams help you develop resilience
- Dreams lead you to the solutions for transforming your pain into abundance

## *Dreams give you a sense of purpose and fulfillment*

Dreams and purpose are intrinsically connected. A dream not only gives your life meaning but also provides a compelling reason to get out of bed each day. It fuels your passion, ignites your drive, and offers a sense of fulfillment. The pursuit of your dreams is a journey of personal growth and the realization of your innate potential.

# The Magic of Dreaming

In The Magic of Pain chapter, I shared a story about the dream I had when I was 20 years old, where God spoke to me about pursuing spiritual healing work. This dream has brought me so much growth, healing, and achievement. In pursuit of this dream, I have earned three master's degrees, become an ordained minister, written this book, and developed a business around my dream work. This dream led me to do the healing work I needed on myself to date and marry my husband, Scott. In addition, it has led me to meet many amazing people, develop lifelong friendships, and improve my family life. My dream has also taken me on a profound and unexpected journey of healing and transformation. Continuing to pursue my dream brings greater richness, juiciness, and increasing fulfillment into my life.

Even if you don't achieve your dream, the mere act of pursuing it can be profoundly meaningful. The process itself is an adventure filled with joy, discovery, and satisfaction. The path to the dream is as valuable as reaching the destination because of the growth, accomplishment, and meaning you acquire along the way. There's no actual destination with your big dream, but rather milestones along the way.

### *Dreams stay with you*
In my experience, your big dreams stay with you. You may experience periods in your life that seem to take you far away from your dream, but your dream never leaves you. You may even forget your dream temporarily. When you're ready and open to it, your dream will come back to you.

In 1995, I started studying energy healing and sacred mysteries at the Healing Light Center Church. I had a dream of pursuing the Crucible Program and getting ordained. I studied for many years but didn't apply to the program. Then, in 2003, I got married and became pregnant. My life took a radical turn toward family, raising children, and having a stable job. Unfortunately, it was not until I got a divorce in 2012 that I went back to the idea of pursuing this dream. But because I was struggling as a single mom, working full-time, and going through other life stuff, I didn't return to actively pursuing this dream until 2020. Then, I got ordained from the Crucible Program in 2023. This dream took me 28 years to accomplish, yet it stuck with me.

### *Dreams give you orientation and direction*
No matter how unrealistic it may seem, pursuing your dream provides you with an essential sense of direction. A dream is a spiritual compass that points you toward worthwhile, soulful growth and attainment. Having direction or orientation is about having clarity about what you're pursuing and where you're going. This concept is related to navigating your life. Your dream defines a destination, and then you determine where you are in proximity to the dream. When you tap into your dream to help you establish your course heading, you'll get more clarity on the next steps and concrete goals that will take you in the direction of your dream.

The dream comes first before the forward movement. Sometimes, a dream is at the edge of your reality; you have no idea how you're going to create it, yet you're compelled to achieve this dream. A dream isn't concrete like a goal. It's more like a fuzzy vision or a magnetic sense of what you want. You may not know how you're going to achieve it, but you know deep down it's what you want. Rely on your dreams to help you define what you want.

### *Dreams help you develop resilience*
Your big dream helps you navigate the complexities of life and inspires you to push through challenges and limitations. It fuels

your creativity and determination, making you resilient in the face of adversity. Even when you face setbacks and self-doubt, reconnecting with your dream offers the motivation needed to overcome obstacles.

There have been several times throughout my life that I came to an obstacle and wanted to give up. In some cases, the dream was put on hold for months or even years. If your dream is big and juicy, you'll want to overcome the obstacles to continue. It will inspire you to develop the capacity to endure. The pursuit of a big dream pulls you forward. It equips you with the strength to withstand hardships, rerouting you back to your path when life steers you off course. You must have the desire to chase your dream, but the dream, in turn, gives you an irresistible reason to return to it and persist, even when it appears unattainable.

## *Dreams lead you to the solutions for transforming your pain into abundance*

The connection may not be obvious at first, but your emotional and existential pains are intertwined with your big dream. The pain that motivates you to change is the other side of the coin from the dream. As I have followed the mystery of my big dream to accomplish goals, objectives, and milestones, I have simultaneously been on a journey of healing and transmuting emotional pain to make room for greater abundance.

A big dream is a mystery that connects you to your soul self, which provides you with the solutions to the complexity of your life.

## What is the magic of dreaming big?

There are several types of dreams. The first is the one you experience when you're sleeping, a realm of subconscious imagery, narrative, and communication with your psyche. The second type, daydreams, fill your waking hours with visions, musings, and reverie. The third, the focus of this discussion, is the dream of your life, the grand vision of what you want to create, who you aspire to be, and how you want to live your life.

It's important to distinguish dreams from goals. Dreams are nebulous, expansive, and often defy the boundaries of practicality. Goals, on the other hand, are SMART—Specific, Measurable, Achievable, Realistic, and Time-bound. Big dreams are often indefinite and intangible, whereas goals are concrete and precise. Big dreams could take years or a lifetime to bring to fruition. A goal is an objective you can accomplish in the short- to mid-term. Dreams may not appear realistic or achievable at first, but they're the foundation of innovation and transformation. They challenge you to think beyond your sense of the ordinary and explore your capacity for the extraordinary.

To make a dream realistic, you need to take action and cultivate a burning desire to make it a reality, as discussed in the next chapter. A dream connects you with your higher self and your unique essence. People who live the life of their dreams are connected to a higher sense of purpose, their creativity, and their unique essence. A dream is your soul's calling, your connection to your tremendous potential.

# The Magic of Dreaming

## How do you dream big?

Figuring out what you want may be the most challenging task of this practice. Start where you are now. In many years of teaching this Moon work, I have discovered that many people often don't know what they want. For some, the idea of dreaming has been discouraged throughout their lives due to cultural or personal circumstances. Such discouragement can be stifling, hindering personal growth and aspiration. Big dreams aren't always encouraged in all environments.

I once worked with a woman who grew up in an environment where dreaming was actively discouraged. Her father advised her to keep her head down and work diligently, stifling her dreams. This upbringing left her feeling lost, unable to articulate her dreams as an adult. She had a small business but had difficulty figuring out what direction to take it. She couldn't articulate what she wanted, so she didn't know how to go after it and get what she wanted either.

Your yearning for a dream may be quashed by external factors or childhood experiences, but as an adult, it's crucial for you to rediscover the magic of dreaming. Any dream that excites or inspires you is worth pursuing. You want your dreams to be juicy, exhilarating, and get your blood pumping.

As you do the Moon practices in this book, you'll begin to define and refine your dream, increasing your clarity on what you want. The next chapter on desire has tips to help you when you cannot articulate your dream.

# Activating Lunar Alchemy

For now, here are some tips to warm you up for dreaming big:

- Allow yourself to daydream
- Write your sleeping dreams down
- Write your waking dreams down
- Meditate (my dream ideas often come to me in meditation)
- Ask yourself questions about your dreams and then answer them with free writing

Free writing is a straightforward exercise that helps you get your thoughts flowing and generate ideas. With free writing, you want to access your creativity and bypass your inner critic. There are a few rules for freewriting:

1. Give yourself a quiet space and time to write
2. Write for a set amount of time, such as 10 to 15 minutes
3. Keep your pen moving; don't stop writing
4. Don't worry about grammar, spelling, or punctuation
5. Write whatever comes to mind

Free writing prompts:

- What is my dream work/job/career?
- What is my dream home?
- What is my dream location or destination?
- What is my dream body/health?
- What is my dream relationship?
- What is my dream for feeling connected?

One tool for making your dream a reality is visualization. When my dreams feel far off, I visualize them coming true and how it feels to live these dreams. To make the dream more tangible,

## The Magic of Dreaming

practice daily visualization. Building up this imagery will help you stay connected to your sense of purpose and enthusiasm about achieving the dream. Visualization often leads you to your next actionable step.

Tony Robbins says that visualization helps you build certainty. Professional athletes use visualization to see themselves accomplishing marvelous tasks. Then, they go out and accomplish these incredible athletic feats.

As an artist, I use visualization to create an art piece in my imagination before attempting to create it in real life. I generally have a very clear image in my head before executing an art piece. Visualization is one way to build the dream on the etheric plane. When the vision is concrete in your mind, it's relatively easy to make the plans and take the steps to manifest it physically.

### ACTIONS YOU CAN TAKE AS A RESULT OF READING THIS CHAPTER:

1. Write your dreams down: daydreams, sleep dreams, and aspirational dreams.

2. Practice freewriting in your journal regarding your dreams.

3. Visualize your dreams coming true and listen for the action steps.

# CHAPTER 4

# The Magic of Desire

*"A God of fire is the only one there is. Our God is not like an iceberg but like a forest fire. He is never compared to the moon with its cool glow but rather to the sun, radiating warmth. He dwells in the light of the rising sun. Whatever he does shines brightly and is carried out with burning desire and a blazing purpose."* – Reinhard Bonnke

*"If you're doing this because you feel like you have a burning desire to do it, then you'll find a way to do it, no matter what. If you're doing this because you're thinking, 'Hey, this will be really cool. I'll be famous. I'll*

# Activating Lunar Alchemy

*be on YouTube,' then you'll probably quit, because it's not easy to do for the long haul."*
*– Trisha Yearwood*

*"Be fearless in the pursuit of what sets your soul on fire." – Jennifer Lee*

Now you have a big dream. What enables you to bring that dream into reality?

One of the most magical and powerful tools to make your dreams a reality is having a burning desire:

- Desire moves you to take action—it 'lights a fire under your ass'
- Desire helps you overcome/transmute obstacles
- Desire is magnetic; it attracts resources, synchronicity, and gifts from the Universe
- Desire attunes you to your unique sense of purpose
- Desire leads to the catalytic moment of manifestation

Be honest with yourself. When you really, really want something, you know how to get it, right?! That is the magic of desire.

After I got a divorce, I went through a long period of struggling financially. To supplement my income, I got into network marketing and started selling nutritional supplements.

Because network marketing requires sales, you get a lot of training on putting yourself out there and having a *why* that moves you, etc. There's a lot of talk about how much money you are going to make and the fancy cars you are going to drive. So, like my network marketing colleagues, I set big financial goals and attempted to visualize the fancy cars. But I never did achieve those financial goals.

Around the same time, I began dating (post-divorce). I discovered that I was highly motivated to attract a boyfriend. When I set my mind and energy to the task, I could attract a boyfriend like that (snap of my fingers)!

What I realized was that the desire to have sex moved me. I could move mountains, overcome obstacles, and produce enough energy to accomplish anything.

### *Desire moves you to take action—it 'lights a fire under your ass'*

So, why couldn't I gain the money and reach my financial goals? Because I don't have a burning desire to have money. Even 10 years later, I still have difficulty achieving financial goals when they're just about money. However, if the goal is tied to something I really care about and have a burning desire to achieve, I can come up with the money.

"What about self-discipline? Isn't that what really makes things happen?"

I recently read an article from Tauseef Ahmed Dar, CEO of AdexLearnings. He said that research shows the following:

- Only 8% of people achieve their dreams/goals
- 92% just give up or fail to do it

According to Mr. Dar, discipline and a commitment to achieving your dreams is what makes them a reality. I disagree. Having energy, excitement, and passion day after day requires a burning

## Activating Lunar Alchemy

desire. A burning desire will give you discipline and commitment and help you solve problems and get through the tough times.

In my experience, when you attempt to create a big dream or achieve a goal that's bigger than yourself, your emotional crap comes up. You feel blocked at every turn. You're making progress, and WHAMO! Some major chaotic event happens that uproots your life!

What gets you back on track and helps you put all of the pieces back together? It's desire. Because when you want something so badly, you'll keep coming back to it even after you've been side-tracked.

I started writing this book in 2013. I even bought a publishing package for it (even though I was a broke single mom) because I wanted it that badly. I wrote up all the work, got a website, and published it on my website. Then, I couldn't figure out how to install a 'payment' button on my WordPress site.

In the meantime, I was in deep financial debt. My kids were 3 and 10. I wasn't making enough to cover the mortgage and the bills. So, I took on more work and put this project on hold.

However, the dream of writing this book and teaching this Lunar Alchemy practice kept coming back to me. I kept dreaming of it and visualizing it.

There was a lot of emotional baggage to get rid of. First, I had a voice in my head that would play over and over, saying, 'I'm crazy.' I had to turn off that voice because it was leading me to believe my dreams and work were crazy.

## The Magic of Desire

Then I had layers upon layers of self-doubt, fear, perfectionism, not feeling good enough, not feeling like I knew enough, and shame. But I kept visualizing this book and peeling away these layers and obstacles and seeing them for what they are—just bullshit programming that I took on at some point in my life.

I kept writing drafts of this book, and then before really completing it, a financial crisis or some other crisis would happen, and I would get off track.

### *Desire helps you overcome/transmute obstacles*
Then came the moment this year, after doing the Moon work, visualizing and stoking my desire, and deciding that this was the most important thing to accomplish in life right now, it happened. I started completing my book in earnest.

Now, here it is in your hands!

I had a big dream and stoked that desire for the dream that got me here. Did I do the work? Yes. Did it take discipline? Yes. But I would have never been able to create and maintain the discipline without a burning desire.

After facing a few of these crises and internal obstacles, you realize that what's holding you back is just your self-doubt and resistance. So, what do you do? You tap back into that burning desire. This fires you up! Makes you invincible! And then you're back to it.

## What is desire?

Caroline Casey, author of *Making the Gods Work for You: The Astrological Language of the Psyche*, states the following:

"All desires are pure if we distill them back to their original intention…Desires are our instructional blueprints of the possible."

Remember my story about money versus sex? This is about distilling your desire to its essence, figuring out what really moves or pulls you.

Desire is defined as something long hoped for.[10] It's also defined as a longing or craving. Desire is magnetic, passionate, and attractive. I advise you to stoke that longing rather than reject it.

When you fan the flames of your desire, you'll get to a point where you're unstoppable, and you'll be pulled by attraction to achieve the result of that burning desire.

*Desire is magnetic and attractive, giving you superhuman power to attract resources, synchronicity, and gifts from the Universe.*

## How to stoke your dreams into a burning desire

Do you know how you defined your dream? If yes, visualize that dream coming true, and as you visualize it, feel what it feels like to achieve this dream or desire. Feel all those juicy feelings of accomplishment, joy, and pride. When you visualize with emotion, you can stoke up the fire of desire. When you feel it, it makes it real to you, and you want it more. This is also a good tip for manifestation—visualize the outcome using emotion to supercharge it.

## The Magic of Desire

If you don't know what you desire, that's no problem. You can find and discover what you desire by defining your *core desired emotions*. Your core desired emotions are around five to seven emotional states that really light you up. This concept was created by Danielle LaPorte in her workbook, *The Desire Map*. Your core desired emotions are like an emotional fingerprint; they're unique to you.

For example, mine are inspiration, abundance, radiance, joy, and mystical. These define how I want to feel in my work, health, relationships, spirituality, and other areas of my life.

You can also use the Lunar Alchemy process to help you reveal what you deeply desire. When you do your New Moon wheel, you're going to ask questions about how you want to feel, like:

- How do you want to feel mentally?
- How do you want to feel financially?
- How do you want to feel physically?
- How do you want to feel in your environment?
- How do you want to feel emotionally?
- How do you want to feel in relationships?
- How do you want to feel spiritually?
- How do you want to feel creatively?

As you get answers to these questions, play with the emotions, ponder them, consider them, and test them out. Are these really the emotions that make you feel alive, enthusiastic, and 'on fire'?

After you've defined how you want to feel, return to doing a visualization practice and feel yourself feeling these core desired emotions. As you feel them, what ideas come to you? In my experience, feeling these emotions will show you what you want to do, what you want to act on, and what you want to experience.

When I am feeling lost and disoriented in my life, I return to the core desired emotions. For example, when I visualize and focus on inspiration, ideas come to me about what to do to feel inspired, like reading that particular book, making that painting that I have been thinking of, going to that museum, or taking that class.

If you're languishing in your life, visualizing how you want to feel is a powerful way to bring you back to yourself and stimulate your intrinsic motivation.

### *Desire attunes you to your unique sense of purpose*
As I worked on defining my core desired emotions in 2016, I grappled with how to define what I wanted to feel spiritually. Inspiration is a spiritual state for me, yet I wanted a word that described the feeling of being connected and guided by God. For a while, I tried 'Divine Synchronicity' because when I experienced moments of synchronicity, I felt that connection that I was longing for, and the synchronicities felt like confirmation that I was moving in the right direction. I finally arrived at 'mystical,' which describes the deeper mystery we feel when we're connected to God or a Higher Power.

This core desired emotion of 'mystical' has propelled me in the direction of writing this book. When I visualize feeling *mystical,* I get lots of creative ideas about what I want to learn, classes I want to take in the sacred mysteries, and what I want to write about.

The feeling of being mystical has led me on a sincere journey of growth these past several years. I've studied astrology, gotten

# The Magic of Desire

ordained, developed the Moon Work, taught classes, and so much more.

I urge you to trust the process and tune into how you want to feel so that you can discover your *burning desires*. Then, stoke that desire with visualization and feeling.

## *Desire leads to the catalytic moment of manifestation*

I've been working on developing the method of *Activating Lunar Alchemy* since around 2000 and teaching it since 2018. As I've taught it, I wanted to ensure the tools and techniques would be effective if used and applied.

One of my students, who started studying the Moon Work three years ago, had the desire to write a second book. She used the tools in this book to build her desire, take action, and overcome her obstacles. Her book is a creative work; she played with different ideas for several years. She continued to build her desire and act. As she worked on her project, she got clearer and clearer until finally, last fall, the creative work, writing, and ideas fell into place. All of a sudden, she had the desire to create an Oracle Deck with the accompanying book.

I witnessed her catalytic moment when everything clicked into place. She wrote a mission statement and began to write very consistently until the manuscript was done. She published her Oracle Deck in the spring and began promoting her new deck.

She followed this desire for a long while. She would work on it and be creative. Then, an obstacle would come up, and the work would fall into the background for a while. Then, it would come back to her that what she really wanted to do was write this book. After dancing with that dream and building that desire, finally, the desire to write the book became so intense and compelling that the path of manifestation became clear, and she knew what she wanted to create, and she created it.

When you follow and stoke your desires, they'll lead you to the catalytic moment of manifestation.

## Distilling your desire to its essence

Do you think that you want massive wealth? There's nothing wrong with wanting massive wealth. But is that really what you want in life? I challenge you to dig deeper to distill the desire for wealth down to its essence. Instead, do you really desire a feeling of security? The freedom to travel? Or enough money so that you can do the work you love?

I asked myself what I would do if I had a million dollars, and I realized I wanted to write, publish my books, and teach. Rather than attempting to earn a million dollars, I focused my energy on writing, publishing, and teaching. I can do all those without a million dollars and feel mystical, joyful, inspired, radiant, and abundant while doing that work.

When you distill your desires to their essence, you open up possibilities for yourself. You unleash your resourcefulness to create what it is you really want.

When people are asked whether they would like to be wealthy or make an impact in the world, most people answer that they would like to make an impact. You likely want to lead a meaningful life and make a unique contribution to the world. Following the path of your desire will lead you there.

## ACTIONS YOU CAN TAKE AS A RESULT OF READING THIS CHAPTER:

1. Define your core desire emotions.

2. Practice visualizing your dreams with feeling.

3. Get fired up and take immediate action to achieve your dreams!

# CHAPTER 5

# The Magic of Creativity

*"Creativity is our most powerful tool to shape the world we want to live in."* – Isra Hirsi

*"There is no doubt that creativity is the most important human resource of all. Without creativity, there would be no progress, and we would be forever repeating the same patterns."* – Edward De Bono

*"True alchemy lies in this formula: 'Your memory and your senses are but the nourishment of your creative impulse."* – Arthur Rimbaud

## Activating Lunar Alchemy

The scope of this chapter is about using creativity when creating your Moon Wheels and learning how to leverage your creativity to create the life of your dreams.

You might think of creativity as this precious talent only a lucky few possess, but I disagree. I think to be human is to be creative. You're creative in all of your thoughts, choices, and actions. You change and affect the world around you, and in that, you're immensely creative. Humans are creative in their ability to create life. Humans are creative in thought, word, and deed. Perhaps the word *creativity* has been confused with artistry. You're creative, and your human creative expression can be refined to become art if you decide to put your energy and focus into that.

There are so many benefits to creativity. For the sake of this practice, here are the top five benefits:

- Creativity connects you to the Creator
- Creativity helps you refine your self-expression and authenticity
- Creativity is a superpower that allows you to solve problems and be resourceful and innovative
- Through creativity, you can integrate experiences and make meaningful connections
- Creativity relieves stress and promotes emotional well-being

### *Creativity connects you to the Creator*
As a creator, you're connected to the Creator. It's important for you to know that creativity connects you to the Divine. Your essence is creative. You must create to live, survive, or thrive. You have the power to be creative. Creativity is part of your humanness.

# The Magic of Creativity

In *Thumbs, Toes, and Tears*, Chip Walker explains how the human hand is hard-wired to the brain and that our hands and exceptional thumbs are some of the traits that make us human. There's a synergistic relationship between our hands and brains. Everything we make, sense, or fashion with our hands influences our brain wiring. Our super sensitive hands and unique and extraordinary thumbs make it possible for humans to manipulate the surrounding environment, create tools, and conduct very refined work, like painting the Mona Lisa.

> *Crammed within every square inch of our digits are nine thousand hypersensitive, egg-shaped buds called Meissner's corpuscles, which lay just below the epidermis, our outermost layer of skin. Inside each bud lies coiled nerves that sense and snatch up the signals initiated by whatever we touch and send it to the brain for processing. The physical power and dexterity of our thumbs and hands make them central to our humanity. Their biological evolution literally changed our minds. They enabled us to better manipulate the world around us, and the manipulation of things then came to also mold our minds.*[11]

You're hard-wired to be creative. Using your hands to make something positively affects your brain. As we make things with our hands, we also develop the capacity to be creative and solve more complex problems. The root word for manipulate and manifest is *mani*, which means hand. Through your hands and mind, you have the capacity to create the world around you and make your dreams a reality.

## *Creativity helps you refine your self-expression and authenticity*

It doesn't matter what form it takes; when you're creative, you're expressing yourself and your authenticity. You could be an artist, a writer, or a singer; you could cook, make a spreadsheet, or build a Lego castle; everything you make reflects your creativity and self-expression.

I used to teach art appreciation to college students, which is a general education class, so the students weren't necessarily artists. I gave a 'Show and Tell' assignment at the beginning of each semester. The students had to bring in something they made by hand. Then, they had to analyze it using the elements and design principles of art. It didn't matter what the student made or when. One woman brought in examples of her cake decorating, and another man brought in a chandelier made of Elk antlers. No matter what you make or what medium you use, you're expressing your creativity and authenticity. The very choices you make are part of the creative process.

### *Creativity is a superpower that allows you to solve problems, be resourceful, & innovative*

When you engage your creativity, you engage this amazing problem-solving ability that enables you to be innovative, get things done, or manifest an idea. Let's say, for example, that you make a decision to accomplish something big, complex, and challenging. This could be something that you've never done before. Immediately, you begin to engage your creativity in order to solve that problem; even making the preliminary plan to accomplish this task is a creative process.

Creativity is human and practical magic. Engaging our creativity to solve complex problems or create what we want in life is at the heart of our magical abilities because we use our minds, hands, and frontal lobes to create solutions out of thin air. This is how Elon Musk can build a spaceship to get to Mars—he uses his innate creativity.

# The Magic of Creativity

***Creativity helps you integrate experiences and make meaningful connections***
Often, when you're engaging your creativity, you're engaging both the right and left hemispheres of your brain. This allows you to tap into your analytical abilities and your emotional abilities and integrate them. Doing a creative process can help you synthesize ideas, integrate experiences, and make meaningful connections between different parts of yourself and your brain. Furthermore, stimulating the right brain inspires holistic thinking and making connections.

For my master's thesis, I studied psychology and art to explore and understand the connection between body and spirit. I discovered a way to create self-portraits that would induce a healing in me. It was like I worked through my emotional pain by painting it. I also found that I could paint a healing vision of myself and then move toward that healing vision.

There are a couple of things going on with this creative process that are important to point out. One, I was able to tap into my emotions and traumas in a way that telling my story verbally couldn't accomplish. Two, I found that I could effectively create, heal, change, and transform my life by directing my creative ability toward healing myself. This is one of the ways that the Moon Wheels work as a creative container of the self—you're using your creativity to fashion the life of your dreams and to imagine a more fulfilling life for yourself. You're telling your psyche what you want to be like and feel like, which induces a deep change process.

***Creativity relieves stress and promotes emotional well-being***
I know from anecdotal experience that creative tasks relieve stress and promote emotional well-being. Having taught art for

many years, I've had many students tell me what a joy and relief it is to be creative and spend time in art class.

> *Simply engaging in creative activities can boost your mental health. A new survey from APA found that about half (46%) of Americans use creative activities to relieve stress or anxiety, such as playing the piano, crocheting a blanket, dancing with friends, or solving crossword puzzles. Americans who rate their mental health as very good or excellent tend to engage in creative activities more frequently than those who rate their mental health as fair or poor.*[12]

## What is Creativity?

*Merriam-Webster's Dictionary* says that creativity is 'the ability to create.' Etymologically, *create*, the verb, means:

*to bring into being,' early 15c., from Latin creatus, past participle of creare 'to make, bring forth, produce, procreate, beget, cause,' related to* **Ceres** *and to crescere 'arise, be born, increase, grow,' from PIE root* ***ker-*** *(2) 'to grow.' De Vaan writes that the original meaning of creare 'was 'to make grow', which can still be found in older texts ....' Related: Created; creating.*[13]

The Roman Goddess Ceres is the goddess of the grain and harvest. Her name is related to the root word of create, *ker*. In ancient Rome, she was called upon to make the crops grow to ensure there was enough food and grain abundance to feed the people. She was also called upon for marriage, childbirth, and for ushering in times of peace.

This Moon practice is also about making things grow, bringing them forth, and increasing your abundance. In this work, you're attuning your creative energy to the Moon Cycle's creative energy

## The Magic of Creativity

to make your dreams and desires grow. You grow your dreams, desires and the life you want to live, much the same way you grow a garden: you plant seeds, water, fertilize, and nurture them, and you remove any unwanted weeds that threaten the growth of your dream garden.

I want you to take two things away from this chapter:

1. Leverage your innate creativity to create the life of your dreams. You can effectively do this by following and repeating the four steps of the Moon Cycle process, which are detailed in the following chapters.

2. Use your creativity to imbue your Moon Wheels with your energy, joy, authenticity, and unique magic. Your Moon Wheels are a reflection of you. They're also magical objects that help you concentrate your thoughts, emotions, creativity, dreams, and desires into a cohesive vision for your life. The Moon Wheels will help you refine what you want and lead you to clarity, purpose, balance, healing, and abundance.

Your creativity is a way to bring forth your energy and make something special. When you care about something or someone, you put care and attention into it to make it special. For my last birthday, my daughters made me handmade cards with drawings and lovely notes of love and appreciation. They put their love and care into these cards to show me how important I am to them. Do your Moon Wheels with the same kind of love, care, and creativity to treat your dreams, desires, and yourself as special as you would treat someone you love.

# Activating Lunar Alchemy

## How to apply your Creative Magic in the Moon Work:

Four times in a Moon Cycle, you'll create a Moon Wheel. You'll make one approximately every week for each quarter of the Moon Cycle: New Moon, First Quarter, Full Moon, and Last Quarter. The Moon Wheels are slightly different each quarter because they're designed to attune you to the creative energy of the specific part of the Moon Cycle.

Your Moon Wheels can be positive triggers for your goals, dreams, and desires. Consider what will positively trigger you to keep creating the life of your dreams. For example, I use a lot of color as a positive trigger. I use symbolic imagery as a positive trigger, such as stars, hearts, and simple symbolic drawings. I also use animal totems and animal symbolism, like power animals, to encourage me to keep going.

One Moon Cycle in 2022, I drew an elephant on my New and Full Moon wheels. One of the traits that the elephant symbolizes is being unstoppable. At the time, I really needed the reminder that I'm unstoppable, like the elephant. Every time I see an elephant totem now it reminds me to be unstoppable.

# The Magic of Creativity

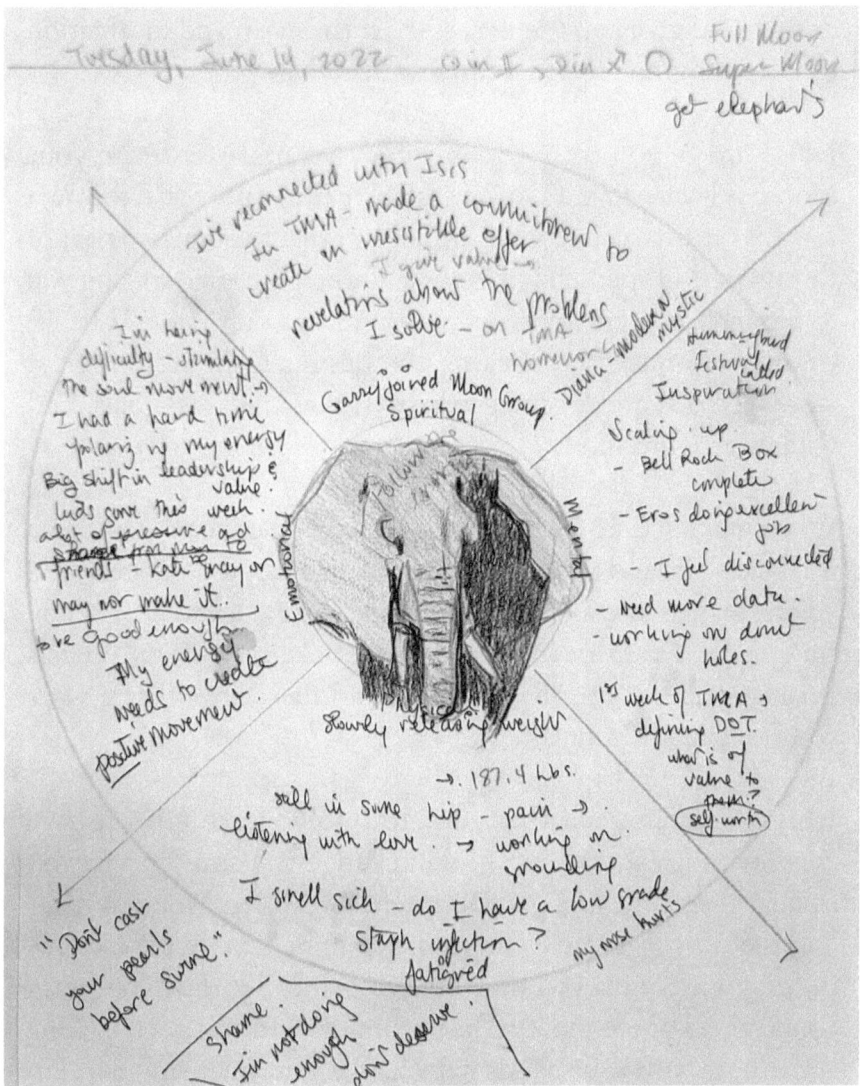

You want your Moon Wheels to empower, inspire, engage, and connect with you. Think about what imagery, shapes, symbols, designs, or colors represent the power and majesty of your biggest dreams and goals. Tap into that inspiration and vision when you create your Moon Wheels. Tapping into your inspiration and vision will connect you with your dreams and desires and give you the necessary enthusiasm and motivation to keep moving toward your dreams.

I discourage you from looking for a formula to create your Moon Wheels. There's an overall structure but not a formula for this creative process. It's important that the creative part of this process is open-ended for you. Rather, I'm encouraging you to tap into your creativity when you make your Moon Wheels, to dig deep into your dreams and desires to figure out what words, colors, and/or images express your dreams, goals, and core desired emotions.

When making the Moon Wheels, some people use poetry; some use keywords and symbolic images; some just use imagery and colors; some write affirmations; some write questions or 'I am' statements. There are infinite ways to make your Moon Wheels because you are an infinite being, and there are infinite ways you can express yourself.

I highly recommend that you tap into your unique creative expression because doing so will change you and support you in changing your life. As you interact with the Moon Wheels and the Moon's creative rhythm, you're in a co-creative dance to bring forth what you want from life. Just like the hand-brain connection I wrote about at the beginning of this chapter, making something with your hands will change your brain and develop your capacity to be more creative.

Ideas for how to get started with your Moon Wheels:

- ★ Start simple
- ★ Have fun
- ★ Play with ideas, colors, images, words, and symbols

## The Magic of Creativity

- ★ Pick a media you enjoy, such as colored pencils, markers, or watercolors
- ★ Add doodles or shapes
- ★ Make the writing follow a pattern, like a mandala
- ★ Add collaged imagery from the internet or magazines

---

**ACTIONS YOU CAN TAKE AS A RESULT OF READING THIS CHAPTER:**

1. View your life as a creative project and use your creativity to make it a reality!

2. Have fun and a playful attitude when making your Moon Wheels.

3. Make your Moon Wheels special, like making something special for a loved one.

# CHAPTER 6

# The Magic of the Moon Wheel

"Happiness is not a matter of intensity but of balance, order, rhythm and harmony." – Thomas Merton

"When you have balance in your life, work becomes an entirely different experience. There is a passion that moves you to a whole new level of fulfillment and gratitude, and that's when you can do your best...for yourself and for others." – Cara Delevingne

## Activating Lunar Alchemy

*"It is the harmony of the diverse parts, their symmetry, their happy balance; in a word it is all that introduces order, all that gives unity, that permits us to see clearly and to comprehend at once both the ensemble and the details." – Henri Poincare*

The Native American Medicine Wheel is the magical container you utilize in *Activating Lunar Alchemy* to crystalize your dreams and desires and to help you reflect within a sacred mirror. My students and practitioners of this work coined the term *Moon Wheel* to describe the ritualistic wheels made in concert with the four phases of the Moon.

The Medicine Wheel is a sacred tool with unlimited applications and an ingenious design. For the sake of the Moon work, the benefits you draw from utilizing the Medicine Wheel include, but are not limited to, the following:

- Restoring balance in your life
- Healing integration of the four parts of self: intellect, body, emotions, and spirit
- Increasing your self-conscious awareness
- Promoting wholeness and holistic health
- Inducing fresh movement and flow

I learned about the Medicine Wheel from Reverend Rosalyn Bruyere of the Healing Light Center Church as part of my spiritual healing studies in the Crucible Program. I have been given permission to teach the Medicine Wheel, which is a great honor and a responsibility I take very seriously.

Learning the Medicine Wheel has been a tremendous healing gift to me. I have learned about it, prayed with it, and applied

# The Magic of the Moon Wheel

it to my life. I have resolved many situations, been increasingly blessed, and have benefited from the balance and healing it has taught me. The Medicine Wheel is a tool that you can use and practice for your whole life and never fully explore all its uses, applications, and mysteries; rather, it becomes deeper and richer with practice.

This chapter isn't a comprehensive examination of the Medicine Wheel. It's limited to using the Medicine Wheel as a sacred and magical circle, a map, a self-portrait, a compass, and a wheel to move you in the direction of your spiritual growth.

In addition to the above uses, the Medicine Wheel can be utilized as a problem-solving tool, prayer format, community organizing structure, timekeeping system, storytelling device, and so much more. The Medicine Wheel can be used to break destructive habits and patterns, such as addictions, in the different quadrants of self—mental, physical, emotional, and spiritual. The Medicine Wheel is a profound healing tool.

For this Moon work, the Medicine Wheel is a tool that you bring inward to create healing internally and bring yourself into dynamic balance.

On one level, the Medicine Wheel is a map. It can be a literal map, including the four cardinal directions. But it's also a map of the self, showing four quadrants—intellect, body, emotions, and spirit. For every quadrant and direction, there's one of four elements: East is the intellect and air element; South is the body and the fire element; West is the emotions and the water element; and North is the Spirit and the earth element. These quadrants are inscribed in a circle, which is the container, the boundary, and the expression of the whole.

## Medicine Wheel

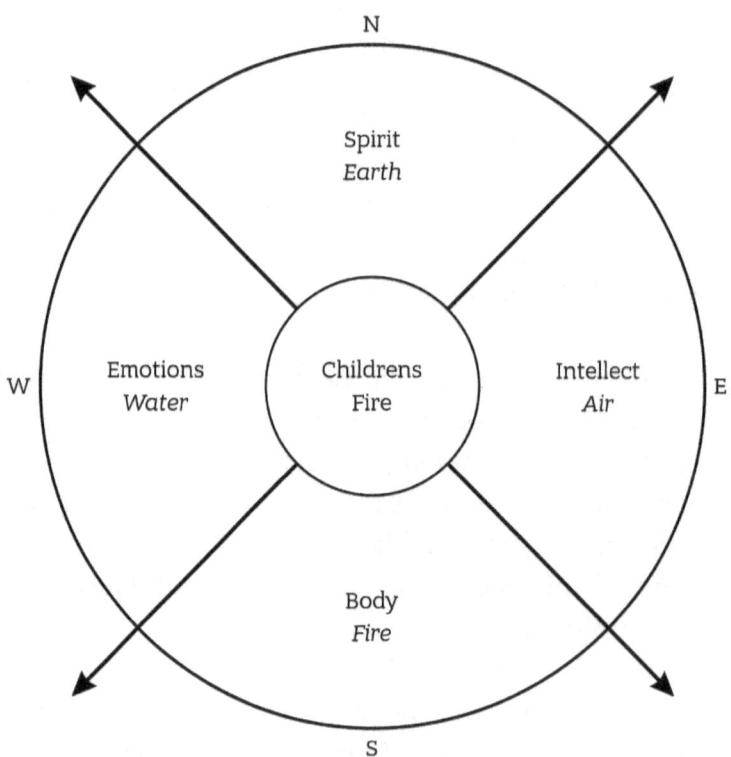

Mathematically, the circle represents one or the whole. In art around the world, across cultures, and throughout history, the circle is a symbol that represents spirit, oneness, community, and the cosmos. It's significant that the Medicine Wheel is in the form of a circle and a wheel. The circle is also a magical container.

The Medicine Wheel also has an inner circle called the Children's Fire. The Children's Fire is at the heart of the Wheel; it's, perhaps, the hub of the wheel. Among First Nations peoples that use the Medicine Wheel to organize the community, the Children's Fire is the center of the community where the very young children are cared for by the elders. Therefore, the Children's Fire represents a place where you gather energy and renewal. As you can imagine, this is a place of high energy, joy, comfort, safety, and centering.

The Medicine Wheel is also a tool to create movement and momentum in your life. First, it's a wheel, which implies that it's used for ease of movement. In this work, you pair the benefits of the Medicine Wheel with the creative rhythm of the Moon cycle, which generates movement in your life. The movement you create relates to the balance and integration that's possible with the Medicine Wheel.

In this process, you'll use the Medicine Wheel for the New Moon and the Full Moon rituals. Then, you'll use a modified wheel to attune to the First Quarter and Last Quarter Moons. Before you begin to pair the wheels in attuning to the Moon cycle, I suggest you make your first Medicine Wheel as a dream map to give you inspiration, energy, and spiritual direction.

## Making Your First Medicine Wheel

For your first project, you're going to make a Medicine Wheel that's like a vision board or a treasure map, although it'll be in wheel form. For this Medicine Wheel, tap into your big dreams to make a map with beautiful and uplifting imagery that motivates you. Also, add your *core desired emotions* because how you want to feel is a very significant part of the process of creating the life of your dreams. Use key words and phrases that speak about your dreams and goals.

# Activating Lunar Alchemy

For example, my dream wheels often include beautiful beach destinations because I love to travel to the ocean. I add my core desired emotions in each quadrant. I also like to use a lot of color and paint to personalize my wheel.

## Medicine Wheel: Dream Map

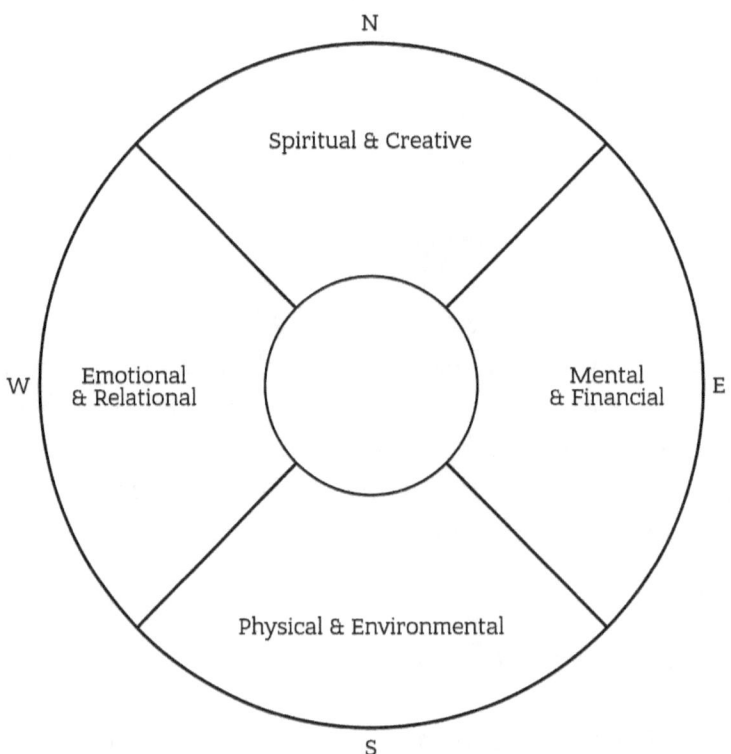

The Wheel is divided into four quadrants plus the center circle, Children's Fire. Play with how to divide your life and dreams into the four mental, physical, emotional, and spiritual quadrants. Of course, these parts of self overlap and interact. Remember that the circle represents the whole, so ultimately, you're addressing your whole self.

# The Magic of the Moon Wheel

In the mental quadrant, I often put mental work and financial goals. In the physical quadrant, I consider my physical body, health, and living environment, such as my home. In the emotional quadrant, I put both the emotional attributes that I desire and also the kinds of relationships I want to create or improve. I put spiritual desires and creative matters in the spiritual quadrant because creativity ties us to the Creator.

If there are other areas of your life I haven't listed above, use your creativity and intuition to determine where to put them in your wheel.

**Supplies:**
11 x 14 drawing paper
Pencil
Compass or large circular objects to draw your circles
Ruler
Makers, colored pencils, paint (optional)
Magazine clippings, photos, or other images (optional)
Glue (optional)

1. Using your compass, draw a small circle for the Children's Fire, using the Dream Map diagram as a guide.
2. Then, draw a large circle that takes up most of your paper.
3. Take your ruler and draw two diagonal lines that intersect with the center of your circles.
4. Outside of the larger circle, mark the cardinal directions: East on the right of the wheel, South at the bottom of the wheel, West on the left of the wheel, and North at the top of the wheel.
5. Then, label each of the four quadrants: 'Mental' in the East, 'Physical' in the South, 'Emotional' in the West, and 'Spiritual' in the North.

## Activating Lunar Alchemy

6. Use your creativity and intuition to fill this wheel with what you want to create in your life. You can draw, write, or paste pictures into your wheel. It's important that you make a wheel that speaks to you and reflects your creativity.
7. Have fun!!

People frequently ask me the best way to phrase what they put in their Medicine Wheel. Do you use affirmations, phrases, or sentences? Do you write the phrases in past, present, or future tense?

I don't have a specific answer. First, I recommend playing with the wheels and seeing what works for you. If affirmations work for you and you're drawn to them, use affirmations. I, personally, do a variety of writing in my Moon Wheels. I write my core desired emotions, add keywords, and write phrases, affirmations, and SMART goals. It really depends on what I'm focused on at the time. Occasionally, I put questions in my Medicine Wheel, especially complex life questions I'm seeking answers to. In some wheels, I put in just imagery with no words.

Some of the other people who have practiced this Moon work very successfully use poetry in their Moon Wheels. Still, others use a variety of keywords. Some people make little symbolic sketches or diagrams to create their wheels.

The Medicine Wheel is a creative tool. It's very important that you draw upon your own creativity to make your wheels. Use words, images, and colors that speak to your psyche and spirit.

It's not advisable to do your wheel in a formulaic way. Making your Medicine Wheel isn't like working with a magical spell.

## The Magic of the Moon Wheel

Rather, the Moon work with the Medicine Wheel is a creative and internal process. In addition, it can be a positive trigger to help guide you toward the outcomes you're seeking. The magic that happens in moon work happens inside of you.

> **ACTIONS YOU CAN TAKE AS A RESULT OF READING THIS CHAPTER:**
>
> 1. Make your Dream Map.

# CHAPTER 7

# The Magic of Seeding the Moon

*"Without a dream, a conscious goal, or a strong intention to go in a specific direction, life is like being in a boat without a rudder- we are thrown capriciously by the waves."*
– Jan Spiller, *New Moon Astrology*

"Timing is everything. When we plant seeds in the springtime, the laws of nature bring about a bountiful crop in the fall. The same seeds planted in a winter snowstorm will likely not yield results, or the results

## Activating Lunar Alchemy

*may require much more hard work and be straggly compared to seeds planted at the appropriate time."*
*– Jan Spiller*

*"In the right light, at the right time, everything is extraordinary." – Aaron Rose*

The symbolic beginning of this alchemical lunar process is attuning to the New Moon through a practice called 'seeding the Moon.' Seeding the Moon is gaining popularity among people seeking to connect with the mystical power of the Moon. Seeding the New Moon with your dreams, wishes, desires, intentions, goals, or affirmations is a potent manifestation practice.

The benefits of attuning to the New Moon are the following:

- Harness the creativity and fertility of the Moon cycle
- Utilize potent timing for manifestation
- Initiate new endeavors with ease
- Begin a process of transformation
- Restore balance

### Harness the creativity and fertility of the Moon cycle

Astrologically, the New Moon is considered the most fertile time to 'seed your dreams.' This is the time of the month when the Earth, Moon, and Sun line up in the sky with the Moon in the middle, making the Moon invisible to the observer on Earth. Farmers who garden by the Moon literally seed annuals during the New Moon or early in the Moon's cycle for the best yields. The energy of the Sun and Moon coming together in the sky approximately every 29 and a half days is creative. I like to think that the Sun, representing our higher self, is imparting a gift or blessing to the Moon, our emotional self, to be brought

## The Magic of Seeding the Moon

to fruition. The Moon, with its regular monthly rhythm, is very creative and often associated with fertility.

### *Utilize potent timing for manifestation*
When you seed the Moon at the New Moon, the energy begins to build with the waxing energy of the Moon. The New Moon begins the Moon cycle and the growth toward the Full Moon. You seed the Moon in the fertile darkness, much like planting a seed into the ground. Then, the waxing of the Moon increases that energy eventually supporting you to act, cultivate your seeds, and bring your seedlings to fruition.

### *Initiate new endeavors with ease*
The New Moon is considered the beginning of a 29-day Moon cycle. It's also the beginning of a three-year creative cycle. In addition, a new moon is the beginning of a 19-year cycle called the Saros Cycle, in which the Sun and Moon form similar patterns in the sky. Consider each New Moon as a powerful new beginning and perfect timing for initiating your dreams and goals. Ideas and projects initiated on the New Moon will be met with rapid growth.

By getting in sync with the Moon cycle, you're working with one of the natural rhythms and energies of the Earth. Attuning to the Moon cycle makes your work easier because you're going with the flow and working with the energy already there. This takes surrendering to and working with the timing to achieve bigger and faster results. To surrender, let go of your fear and your need to control.

### *Begin a process of transformation*
This work is about attuning your energy and focus with the Moon cycle for your healing and growth. Each New Moon is

an opportunity to create what you want with your life. It's an ideal time to launch a project, start a business, begin a new diet or health regime, or institute changes in your life.

On some New Moons, I start completely new practices, like taking up a new exercise routine or spiritual practice. I seed the Moon with these ideas and plans because I want them to increase and be fruitful endeavors for me. I also re-seed what I'm already working on to keep the energy and the focus flowing. For example, as I write this book, I'm seeding the Moon with it every month. This may go on for months (or even years) as I move through different stages of the book, including writing, editing, publishing, and marketing. As you begin new projects and set dreams into motion, you're also setting your own transformative process into motion.

### *Restore balance*
We don't see the Moon for about three days as it approaches the Sun, lines up with the Sun, and then begins a New Moon cycle. In my experience, the vital energy feels lowest at the New Moon. I tend to sleep more and be more tired during this time each month. The New Moon calls you to go inward and spend time listening and being introspective.

It's important to honor this rhythm because you may need more rest. Our culture in the United States is very outward-focused, yang, and productivity-minded. The Moon rhythm is a great tool for teaching you how to go inward, be yin, and rest and restore balance between outward and inward, productivity and rest, external and internal, yang and yin. The energy is concentrated on the New Moon. This concentration is best used in meditation, listening, and going inward.

The Magic of Seeding the Moon

## What is the Magic of the New Moon?

The Moon is always viewed in relationship to the Sun, as well as its relationship to you experiencing the Moon from Earth. On the New Moon, we don't see the Moon because it passes between you and the Sun; the Moon is hidden or invisible for a couple of days.

In astrology, the Sun symbolizes your essential self. You might think of your Sun sign in astrology and consider personality traits central to your birth sign. The Sun also represents your conscious self, the present self, and your higher potential.

In contrast, the Moon represents your emotions, the subconscious self, and the past self. The Moon's rhythm inspires the ebb and flow of dreams, ideas, challenges, and memories coming to the surface. The Moon connects you with the past and helps you process psychical stuff that emerges from the depths of your soul.

At the New Moon, the Sun and Moon form a conjunction. When they're lined up in the sky, it's as if the Sun and Moon are in consensus. In other words, your higher self and your emotional self are in alignment. They're starting a new cycle and want to create something together. Dion Fortune says you can access the superconscious self when the conscious and subconscious selves align.

It's your job in this work to listen to what your higher self and your emotional self want. What do they want to create? What can they both get behind for your best life? These are the dreams and desires to seed at the New Moon. Your higher self is telling you what you want and need. You may hear that voice clearly, or

## Activating Lunar Alchemy

it may take some work to begin to hear your higher self speaking to you. This Moon work will help you develop this ability.

To create the life of your dreams generally flies in the face of what you have been taught about life growing up. You'll find happiness, joy, and inner peace when you listen beyond the negative chatter in your head to hear your soul's calling. This Moon work is about listening to it, writing it down and seeding it in your New Moon wheel, taking action on it (First Quarter), observing what is happening with it (Full Moon), and letting go of any negativity, resistance, or obstacles that have been in your way of creating that dream.

Ultimately, this work is about attunement to your higher self and living the most satisfying and joyful life possible.

At first, this Moon work requires some faith and surrender as you re-align yourself with the timing of the lunar and solar cycles, as well as attuning yourself to the energetic rhythm of the Earth. The Earth's magnetosphere is affected by the mutual rotation of the Moon, the Earth, and the cyclical rhythm created by the Earth revolving around the Sun, yielding the Moon cycle. Your energy field is influenced by the Earth's energy and rhythm.

At first, you'll be artificially attuning your energy to the Moon. However, if you do this practice long enough, you'll realize that you're already a part of the cosmic dance and that this lunar timing is part of the fabric of your psyche, beingness, and energy field. It's an evolutionary process, and it takes work. Yet, the reward of this work is living an extraordinary life of spiritual abundance.

# The Magic of Seeding the Moon

## How to seed the Moon?

Manifestation and spiritual growth are two sides of the same coin.

To attune to the New Moon, give yourself some personal time to be alone and to listen to what you really want. Listen to your dreams. Listen to your guides. Meditate and listen to your higher self. These impulses, inklings, or callings are guiding you to your Soul's potential.

Then, you're going to write and/or draw these 'seeds' into your New Moon wheel.

### New Moon: Seed Your Dreams

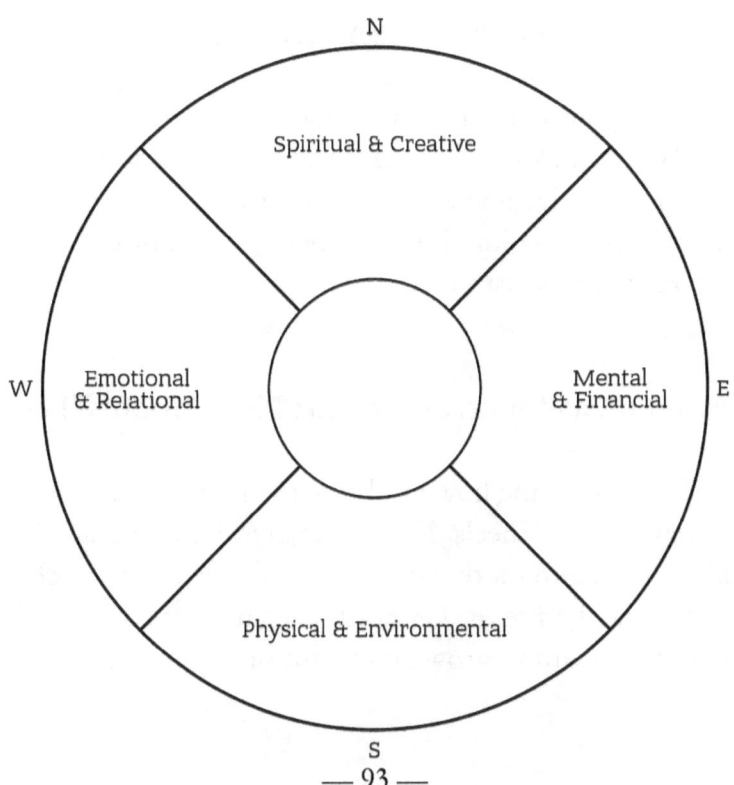

# Activating Lunar Alchemy

**Supplies:**
**11 x 14 paper**
**Pencil**
**Compass or large circle to trace**
**Ruler**
**Paint, markers, colored pencils, other art supplies**

1. Make some sacred time for yourself to make your New Moon wheel
2. Light a candle
3. Invite your higher self in and get into a space of receptivity or listening
4. Draw your New Moon wheel like the diagram
5. Label the four parts of self: mental (East), physical (South), emotional (West), and spiritual (North)
6. Tap into your big dreams and goals
7. Use how you want to feel—the power of emotion—to guide you in this process
8. Add your core desired emotions
9. Write and/or draw your dreams, desires, and goals
10. Get creative and express your visionary energy
11. Use paint, colored pencils, pens, glitter, or collage
12. Have FUN with it

## Tips and ideas for creating your New Moon Wheel

People have asked me how to phrase their dreams and goals in their New Moon Wheels. I use a variety of techniques. If I'm working on seeding a dream that seems far out of reach and appears vague. I write the keywords and emotions of this dream to allow the dream to grow and manifest organically.

## The Magic of Seeding the Moon

I write my core desired emotions in my wheel. They're single emotional words, such as "joy." I do this in my New Moon Wheel because I want to increase the experiences that lead me to feel my core desired emotions.

When I am working on a SMART goal, I write it in my New Moon Wheel as I want to seed that energy and accomplish the goal quickly and efficiently.

I have also written words and phrases in my New Moon Wheel, as well as affirmations and wishes.

There have been months where I only drew images with color in my wheel because I could tap into the imagery and energy but not articulate what I wanted.

In my online Moon group, one of my colleagues draws an animal spirit card for the group. If this animal totem resonates with what I'm working on, I often draw it into my New Moon wheel.

# Activating Lunar Alchemy

The most important aspect of this New Moon ritual and in seeding your New Moon wheel is that you listen to your higher self. Listen for your dreams and desires and capture them in some way on paper. It can be in writing, imagery, or both. It's also important for you to express your own creativity because this work is about you creating the life of your dreams.

# The Magic of Seeding the Moon

I have a student who's a writer, and she puts beautiful poetry and expressive language in her New Moon wheels. They're very eloquent. She's expressing her authenticity and creativity in her New Moon wheels.

Be as specific as possible with what you want in your New Moon wheel. When expressing what you want, consider how you want to feel and write it down.

One time, I asked God for a boyfriend. I wanted him to look a certain way and be into engineering. I received what I asked for. This guy was great and a good guy; however, I quickly discovered that I wasn't attracted to him. It didn't work out between us, but it taught me an important lesson about manifestation.

Sometimes, you get what you want and what you asked for, but it's not quite right. Congratulations! This is evidence that you can manifest what you have asked for.

To remedy this, you need to balance being specific with how you want to feel. For example, you want to attract a significant other. What do you want to feel in this relationship? Love, intimacy, security? How you want to feel in the relationship is the most important aspect of creating what you desire.

**ACTIONS YOU CAN TAKE AS A RESULT OF READING THIS CHAPTER:**

1. To attune to the New Moon, take time to listen to your higher self.

2. Pay attention to what you want and write it down.

3. Make a New Moon Wheel.

# CHAPTER 8

# The Magic of Supportive Action

"Vision without action is a daydream. Action without vision is a nightmare." – Japanese Proverb

"All our dreams can come true, if we have the courage to pursue them." – Walt Disney

"As soon as you start to pursue a dream, your life wakes up and everything has meaning."
– Barbara Sher

## Activating Lunar Alchemy

In US culture, we are all about action, productivity, and making it happen. For the sake of this Moon practice, you learn to balance taking action toward your dreams and goals with listening, observing, and releasing your obstacles. One of the *magics* of this Moon work is its rhythm. It's receptive, then active, receptive, then active. There's a balance in this rhythm, much like our breath—a balance between inhaling and exhaling.

Taking supportive action toward your dreams is critically important; however, do it in a balanced way with listening and receptivity. There's no need to control your life through excessive action. Let go of the control, take action that supports your dreams and goals, and then allow the energy to build and manifest.

Ultimately, by attuning to the Moon cycle, creating what you want will come more easily to you. You won't have to overpower it to make it happen. Let it happen by being in sync with the creative energies that are already all around you.

I'm a recovering workaholic. I spend most of my time and energy doing mental work and spiritual work. I have heard that I'm 'in my head.' It takes a conscious decision on my part to increase the time and energy I put into my health and fitness (eating and exercising), as well as being very deliberate about making time for my husband and family.

As a result of doing this Moon Work for many years, I have begun to let go of the urgency (fear of running out of time) and scarcity (fear of running out of resources) that have compelled me to work seven days a week. These fears have justified being a workaholic for some time. However, as I have worked to create greater balance in my life, I've also found that my abundance and

# The Magic of Supportive Action

free time have increased. I'm more productive and prosperous when I pay attention to all four parts of myself.

You don't need to overact or overreact. Take supportive actions and put time, energy, and attention into your dreams and desires.

The benefits of taking supportive action are the following:

- Taking supportive action directly moves you toward your dreams.
- Taking supportive action tells the Universe you're ready to receive what you're asking for, and support is sent.
- Taking supportive action brings up your resistance from your subconsciousness to your conscious awareness, which allows you to see it and overcome it!
- Taking supportive action brings clarity.

Why do I say supportive action? We can fill our lives with actions and tasks, yet not all actions are the right actions at the right time.

In 2015, I wrote down a powerful dream to get into a long-term relationship with a significant other. I was very clear on how I wanted to feel in this relationship. I wanted to feel secure in the relationship, have love, companionship, emotional intimacy, and be with a securely attached person.

I had an 'anxious attached' attachment style, so when I got into a relationship, I would hold on for dear life. For many years, I would quickly extinguish the relationship's spark because of my grasping, holding, neediness, and fear of losing the love.

Shortly after writing this clear dream of a relationship, I realized I needed to be single for a while and break the grip of the 'anxious attachment' trap I kept getting myself into. At that time, the supportive action for me was to be single and focus on healing myself from this addictive attachment pattern. This healing process took about two years.

After the two years, I realized I was ready to date again and put myself out there in a new way. I started dating more appropriate men. The supportive action at that time was to date and watch for signs of dating securely attached men. Also, as I began dating again, I watched for the signs of the 'avoidant attached' men so I could cut these addictive attachments off early. This worked! In 2017, I started dating Scott, who is securely attached. We dated for several years, started a business together, and got married in 2022.

The point is, I figured out what I wanted and then started taking supportive action to achieve it. The first action was to release the old relationship habit pattern. Another supportive action was to cultivate secure relationships and long-term relationships. At one point, the supportive action was dating and putting myself out there. Then, I achieved what I was attempting to create—a long-term, loving, romantic partnership.

The change happened within. I took external action; however, the preparation I did to achieve this relationship happened inside me. I did a lot of healing and self-work to be comfortable in a secure, loving, and intimate relationship.

### *Taking Supportive Action directly moves you toward your dreams.*

The reason why business gurus are always telling you to take action, take massive action, and so forth is because taking action literally moves you in the direction of your dreams. I'm a

# The Magic of Supportive Action

wholehearted advocate for *taking action*. Yet I say, "Take the right action at the right time to be strategic and conserve your energy." If you're taking massive action and not paying attention to the energy you're creating, you could burn yourself out. There's a time for acting and a time for resting. A time for external work and a time for internal work. A time to give and a time to receive.

***Taking supportive action tells the Universe you're ready to receive what you're asking for, and support is sent.***
Another magic of taking supportive action is that the Universe responds to you and your efforts. When you take supportive actions toward your dreams and desires, you're signifying to God, your Guides, and the Universe that you're ready to receive what you're asking for. Mysterious and timely help is sent. An unforeseen opportunity suddenly appears. You have a synchronous meeting that opens the next step for you. When this happens, it's truly magical and divine.

I believe God helps those who help themselves. You can ask for something in your New Moon Wheel, but if you just wait around to receive it, it probably won't happen. When you take action toward your dreams, you're making a definitive statement to God that you're willing to do the work. You're signaling your intentions to make it a reality. And the Universe delivers.

***Taking supportive action brings up your resistance from your subconsciousness to your conscious awareness, which allows you to see it and overcome it!***
There's another magic of taking supportive action that you may not want. This magic is powerful and very useful for your quest for spiritual abundance. When you start taking supportive action to create something you truly desire, something that stretches you, your resistance will come up. This resistance might take

the form of fear or shame. It might take the form of a behavior pattern, such as procrastination. Perhaps you're dreaming of creating a new business endeavor, and you find yourself watching Netflix all day.

You can go for years, or your whole life without seeing the patterns and behaviors called 'resistance.' When you start taking supportive actions on your dreams and stretching yourself out of your comfort zone, your shit will come up. This is great and a cause for celebration! Woohoo!

When you begin to see your resistance and see it for what it is, you're on the verge of releasing its hold over you. This is the moment when you claim power over your trauma, emotional patterns, and limiting beliefs. Until you see and acknowledge the resistance, it remains in your subconscious and has an invisible hold over you. Being able to see, acknowledge, feel, and identify it is also the moment when you can decide to release it.

Challenging yourself to act, facing your resistance and gently releasing it when it comes up is one of the most important aspects of Lunar Alchemy. I have changed some deep-seated beliefs, emotions, and behavior patterns because I took supportive action and was willing to come up against my resistance. I have struggled with imposter syndrome, fear of being visible and vulnerable, and deep shame about being unworthy. I consider these big, painful emotional blocks. When these energy patterns come up, I work on them and work through them; all the while, I'm committed to making my dream happen. I use my dream and burning desire to give me the purpose, courage, and determination to work through the painful resistance.

# The Magic of Supportive Action

***Taking action brings clarity.***
I recently learned that 'action' brings clarity. Many of my former students have commented on how the Moon work brings them clarity.

Marie Forleo, an entrepreneur, thought leader, and founder of B-School, says, "Clarity comes from engagement, not thought."

She talks about how to engage with what you want to see if it's for you. In other words, when you engage with your dream and take relevant and supportive action toward it, you'll quickly feel whether it is right for you or not. This kind of visceral clarity only comes with engagement and interaction with what you want to create.

At the end of March 2020, when the pandemic shutdown was taking full effect, my husband Scott had the idea to use our laser cutter to cut fabric for a local organization that was sewing surgical masks and other PPE for the hospital. We made a partnership agreement with this non-profit and went to the studio to get to work. Initially, I was very excited about this idea, and I was happy that we were making a contribution to our community.

After we received the sewing pattern and modified it for our laser, Scott and I began cutting masks and preparing them for the seamstresses. Quickly, I became deflated. I didn't enjoy standing in the studio doing this kind of repetitive task. It became obvious to Scott and me that this was not the best use of my skills.

Rather than give up on the project, I decided to put the word out to our community and ask for volunteers. Within a few weeks, we had a team of 16 volunteers working to cut and prepare the mask fabric. At that time, many people wanted to contribute and make a difference.

Within another month, the hospital was so appreciative of our work and the work of the sewing organization that they offered to pay us for these masks. We cut over 20,000 masks in two months and were able to pay our volunteers for their service and keep people gainfully employed for several months during the early pandemic.

The point of this story is that we had a dream and a vision to help the community by cutting this mask material. I did it for a day or two, and I viscerally discovered that I didn't enjoy the repetitive work of cutting these masks. This gave me the clarity that I didn't want to do all of the cutting and work myself. I didn't give up on the dream; however, I pivoted and organized a team of volunteers instead, which kept me quite busy for several months. In the end, we achieved our vision and surpassed our goals and expectations for what was possible. We got paid and paid 16 other people, which we didn't expect or plan for.

## What is supportive action?

On one hand, taking supportive action is taking the next, most obvious step toward the dream you want to create. It also entails doing the right action at the right time to support the growth of the endeavor you're committed to.

How do you know what the right action at the right time is?

In our art business, Scott and I are really busy in November and December for the holidays. To have a successful and prosperous

## The Magic of Supportive Action

holiday season, taking supportive action is working in September and October to gather enough inventory that can take us through the busy holiday season.

In contrast, regarding relationships, this week is Thanksgiving, and my kids are here. My top goal is to edit my book, but I will schedule it around family activities.

It's important to keep in mind what you really want to create and then streamline and prioritize your actions around it.

Here are some questions to ask yourself to help you determine supportive action:

- ➢ Where is the Moon? This question helps me get into balance and in sync with timing.

I consider the Moon cycle and the seasons when I think about what I am creating. I use the waxing moon's upbuilding energy to create and the waning moon's downbuilding and shedding energy to release. This may sound counterintuitive, but aligning my actions with the Moon cycle gives me powerful momentum and helps me conserve and direct my creative energy. As a result, new projects and creative projects come together relatively quickly.

- ➢ Consider your dreams and desires—what are they? Look at your New Moon wheel. What's next?

When figuring out supportive actions at the First Quarter Moon, I review my dreams and desires and look back to my New Moon Wheel. Then, I ask myself, "What's the next, best step in creating that specific dream?"

## Activating Lunar Alchemy

When I ask myself these questions, I get into a state of listening to my higher self and my guides. Sometimes, the next, best step isn't what my rational mind would come up with.

For example, this week is Thanksgiving in the US. I was feeling determined to write and edit every day, despite the holiday and the family time. When I sat down to do my First Quarter Wheel, I heard take Thanksgiving off, rest, and hang out with your family. This may seem obvious to you, but for me, it was a revelation that I would still get this project done if I took a day off!

> ➢ What do you need right now?

This Moon work is very gentle. The Moon and Spirit are patient with us. Consider what you need. For example, do you need more self-care? Do you need to take a class? Do you need to do some healing for yourself? The purpose of this work is to give you a process and framework for living your best life. Allow yourself to ask for what you need and then allow yourself to receive it.

> ➢ What do you want?

At the New Moon, you seed your Moon Wheel with what you want, including your dreams and desires. Continue to ask yourself, "What do I want?" Then, take time to consider what supportive actions are needed to achieve that. What you want may get clearer and more refined as you do this Moon work. As you achieve your dreams and goals, you'll define more or different wants and desires. In addition, you change and grow throughout your life, so your wants also change.

> ➢ Is this supportive action moving me forward?

# The Magic of Supportive Action

There have been times when I have been busy and done tasks just for the sake of being busy. It's important to consider your dream and what you want, then determine the next best step or goal to move you forward.

A few years ago, I made a commitment to a dream to serve 1,000,000 people with my spiritual work. After making this commitment, I realized writing this book was one of the next most important steps. I started my writing project and did a lot of work on this book. Then I realized before I was ready to complete and publish this book, I wanted to finish the Crucible Program and get ordained. After I got ordained, finishing my book became my foremost priority.

As I pursue this dream of serving 1,000,000 people, I focus on one big goal at a time and then prioritize my time around accomplishing that goal. I also organize my daily routines and habits around accomplishing these shorter-term goals.

> ➢ What is your New Moon Wheel telling you? Do you need more rest, rejuvenation and balance right now?

I am suggesting here that you may need more rest, self-care, and mental rejuvenation. As I have grown, healed, and worked through some of my childhood trauma, I've found that I'm still worthy, even if I'm not working seven days a week. Doing less could be the key to moving forward faster on your dreams and desires.

> ➢ Is it time to let go of control and surrender?

I'm a hard worker, a striver, and a survivor. A lot of what I have accomplished has been through hard work, perseverance, and

## Activating Lunar Alchemy

diligence. However, many of the major breakthroughs I have made in my life, and perhaps the most memorable and most powerful breakthroughs, have happened when I surrendered to a higher power or surrendered my control over a situation.

I wholeheartedly advocate striving for your dreams and then balancing that striving with surrender. Surrendering and letting go of your control allows Spirit to step in and help you. Surrendering also opens you up to be receptive to receiving help and guidance from the Divine.

I now ask for the help and guidance I'm seeking to work on my dreams. I ask for help with the next steps. I ask for guidance. I ask for what I need and want. Spirit often tells me to let go, let God, and surrender. By doing this, I'm making a way for God to deliver what I'm asking for. Often, I receive something bigger and better than what I've asked for.

> ➢ Is it time to take an uncomfortable action and put yourself out there in a new way?

Supportive action is often uncomfortable action. If you're attempting to create a new dream or desire that you haven't had success with before, you're going to have to grow in order to manifest or receive that dream. Growth frequently entails doing things differently and getting out of your comfort zone.

A few years ago, I learned at a personal development seminar that I kept myself safe by being invisible. As I stood in front of a room of 70 people and was called out on my invisibility, I cried heavily. It was very painful to be seen in this way and confront the painful childhood story that contributed to my wanting to hide and remain unseen.

# The Magic of Supportive Action

Yet, my dream is to serve 1,000,000 people with my spiritual work and to be a spiritual leader. Can I do that and remain invisible? For me, uncomfortable action and supportive action often mean putting myself out there in an uncomfortable way, either through social media or public events. Every time I do this type of uncomfortable action, I grow and get more confident, as well as move my work and dream forward.

## How to make your First Quarter Wheel

First Quarter: Taking Supportive Actions

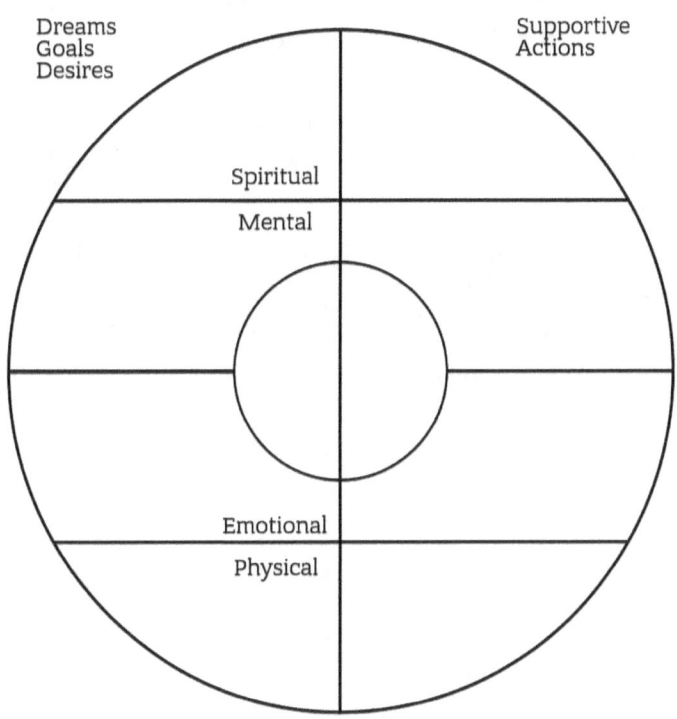

# Activating Lunar Alchemy

**Supplies:**
**11 x 14 paper**
**Pencil**
**Compass or large circle to trace**
**Ruler**
**Paint, markers, colored pencils, or other fun art supplies**

1. Make some sacred space and time for yourself
2. Make it special, light a candle or get a glass of wine or cup of tea
3. Draw a First Quarter Moon Wheel based on the diagram
4. Look back at your New Moon wheel
5. Write your New Moon 'seeds' and your dreams on the left side of the wheel
6. Visualize the dream coming true—feel it happening
7. Listen for the next steps and supportive actions using the questions above
8. Brainstorm a list of supportive actions
9. Write down your supportive actions on the right side of the wheel
10. Take the supportive actions and next small steps that are right in front of you
11. Have fun!

# The Magic of Supportive Action

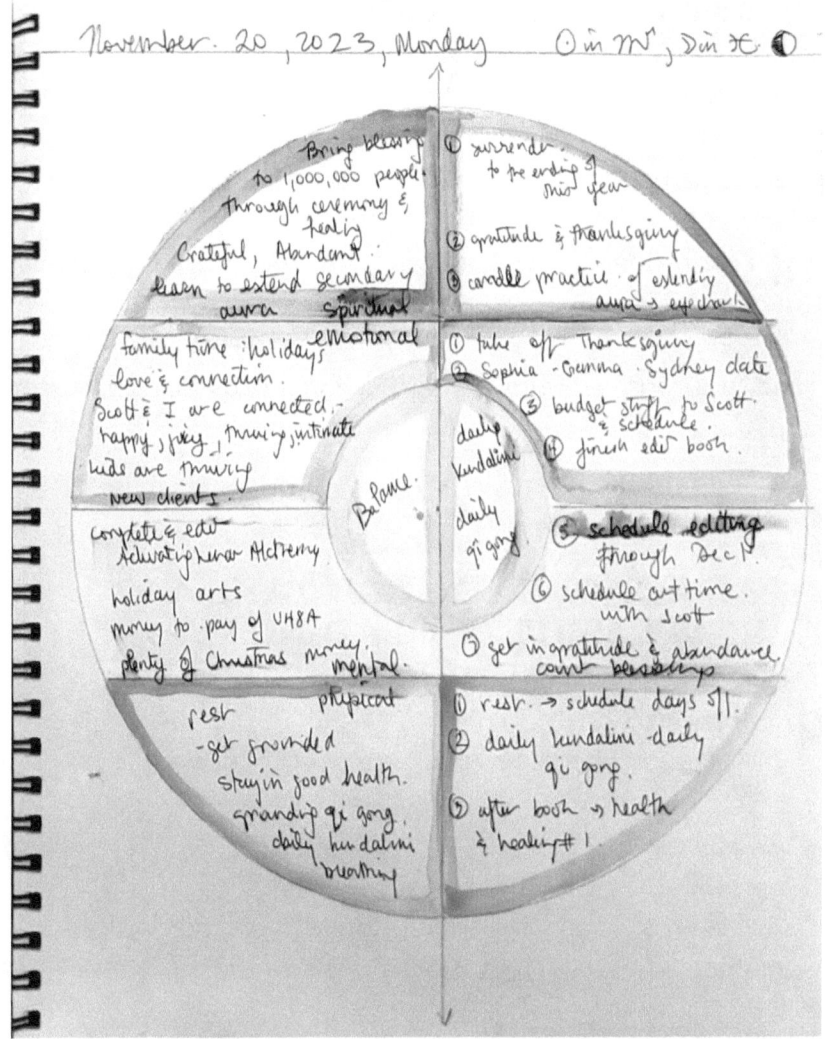

## What if I'm unsure or not decided on my dream?

Start before you're ready. I learned this from Marie Forleo. Pick something that you think you want and start taking action toward it. You'll get more clarity as you take action and work with your dream.

## Activating Lunar Alchemy

You can always change your dream! A New Moon comes approximately every 29 days. Part of this Moon work is observing what's happening. You're going to change and get clearer as you do this work. That means your dream will get clearer and more concrete as you move toward it and act. Just start.

If you really don't know what you want, ask yourself, "How do I want to feel?"

Then, feel those emotions, and they'll tell you what actions to take.

### ACTIONS YOU CAN TAKE AS A RESULT OF READING THIS CHAPTER:

1. Consider whether your actions are supportive or not.

2. Make your First Quarter Moon Wheel.

3. Listen to what's most important to you and do that first.

# CHAPTER 9

# The Magic Mirror

*"When you know yourself, you are empowered. When you accept yourself, you are invincible."* –Tina Lifford

*"Your vision will become clear only when you can look into your own heart. Who looks outside, dreams; who looks inside, awakes."* – Carl Jung

For much of our lives, we experience what's being run by our subconscious and unconscious patterns. We look at the world through the lens of our experiences, including childhood, family, and cultural paradigms. We predominantly act and react from our childhood programming until we increase our conscious

## Activating Lunar Alchemy

awareness of these patterns and programs. With this awareness, we can heal and change these patterns to set ourselves free.

The Full Moon part of Lunar Alchemy takes the most courage in this Moon Cycle work. Yet, if you're willing to be honest with yourself, doing this part of the process is very rewarding and offers tremendous healing, blessings, and valuable insights into yourself and life.

The benefits of attuning to the Full Moon and looking in the Magic Mirror are the following:

- Know thyself—the key to fulfillment
- Become empowered to create the life you desire
- Increase your liberation to live authentically
- Expand your self-conscious awareness
- Make better decisions for yourself
- Increase your self-love, compassion, and self-acceptance

This work is for the courageous among you. Looking at your unconscious patterns and taking responsibility for your healing and growth isn't always easy work. Sometimes, it's hard, painful, raw, and vulnerable. Yet, being able to increase your self-awareness so you can identify and move through internal obstacles is the key to growth and a fulfilling life.

You can have the life you desire and manifest your dreams if you're willing to look within and examine your gifts, strengths, desires, and innate abundance, as well as your fears, pain, shame, and suffering. You access tremendous power when you acknowledge that you're the authority and creator of your own life. With this process, your inner obstacles are opportunities for growth and healing.

# The Magic Mirror

I have big dreams and frequently push myself to create more. As a result, I'm frequently working through emotional challenges, experiencing pain, facing my shadow, and working with my demons in an attempt to make the next evolutionary leap forward. My life and rewards have changed radically as I have taken myself on. I've found that most of my limitations are within. My perceived obstacles are often emotional in nature and lie dormant in my energy field, waiting to be triggered by aspirations of new growth.

If you yearn for healing, change, and growth, this part of the Full Moon work is for you.

## *Know Thyself—the key to fulfillment*
At the Full Moon, you self-reflect with heightened illumination. I call this 'looking in the magic mirror.' Practicing this art of self-reflection at the Full Moon will give you insights into what's really going on with you. This allows you to increasingly create a more fulfilling life and a life of spiritual abundance.

## *Become empowered to create the life you desire*
When you don't know who you are, what you want, or what's holding you back, it's difficult to create the life of your dreams. At the New Moon and First Quarter, you focus your energy on what you want. At the Full Moon, you have the opportunity to look at who you are, what you have accomplished, and what's holding you back. When you begin to know and see your gifts, strengths, and values, you can increase and leverage them to create the life of your dreams. You're empowered even further when you allow yourself to see the subconscious patterns, programs, habits, and behaviors that may be blocking you.

Recently, I had a lot of fear come up. I was making a lot of progress, taking myself on, and then *whamo*, I went into an anxious place. My body was telling me to slow down, and my lower back began to seize up. For several days, I was immobilized and couldn't move because I was in so much pain. At the Full Moon, I looked in the *magic mirror* and saw my scared inner child. I felt alone, insecure, and frightened of taking life on by myself. As I communicated with this inner child, I realized I wasn't alone anymore. I have a loving and supportive husband, family, children, and friends. The people around me want to see me succeed and are helping me to achieve my dreams.

This Full Moon work is about using your insight and intuition to see what's going on within yourself and then seeking the next best path forward. I spent several days after receiving these insights working on my own healing. I did meditations and prayers, I wrote in my journal, and I received deep tissue bodywork to address the physical pain. These insights were painful on some level but also revealing and helpful. I'm now more empowered to address my needs and move forward with my dreams and desires.

### *Increase your liberation to live authentically*
To have real liberty in your life means taking full responsibility for your life and dreams. You may have been victimized in your life, and as a result, you may experience a lot of pain and suffering. In order to change your lot in life, you must be 100% responsible for yourself. At some point, to create what you want out of life, you need to own your past, be present, and work toward the future you desire.

The way that I do this is to view everything in my life as a mirror of myself. The Full Moon is the opportune time to look in the magic mirror to observe yourself, your life, and your results. Following this Moon process will bring forth unconscious patterns to your conscious awareness. Taking responsibility for these patterns and insights gives you increasing freedom and supports you to live from a place of increasing authenticity.

## *Expand your self-conscious awareness*
By practicing this Moon work and self reflecting during the Full Moon, your self-conscious awareness will increase. This is a blessing because you'll begin to see how powerful, creative, and gifted you really are. You'll begin to have an intimate relationship with your dreams and desires and how to achieve them. In time, you'll move through internal obstacles and limitations, and your life will become increasingly blessed, easier, and lighter.

## *Make better decisions for yourself*
If you know what you want and are willing to do what it takes to achieve it, deciding what supports you and what to cut away becomes easier. If you don't know who you are or what you want, it's tempting to stay in indecision and be swept away by the current of your life. Unexpected stuff does happen to you, but how do you respond? Do you let unexpected situations completely derail you from your dreams? Or do you respond and address these challenges head-on because you're committed to what you say you want? These are the day-to-day decisions of life that can lead to your increasing happiness and fulfillment.

## *Increased self-love, compassion, and self-acceptance*
Over the 30 years that I've been seeking healing and growth, I've seen, felt, and experienced a lot of pain, suffering, and darkness in myself. Working through the loss, grief, shame, and fear has rewarded me with immense compassion, as well as self-love and self-acceptance. This is an ongoing process.

You're the product of your time, childhood experiences, DNA, culture, past life experiences, and so forth. These are the limitations you get to work with, work through, and develop. Facing your inner pain and suffering gives you compassion for yourself and others. In addition, as you confront your whole self by looking in the magic mirror, you also develop self-love and self-acceptance.

## What is the Magic of the Full Moon?

At the Full Moon, the face of the Moon you see from Earth is fully illuminated by the Sun. Again, the Sun, Moon, and Earth line up, yet during a Full Moon, the Sun is on one side of the Earth, and the Moon is on the opposite side. In astrology, this aspect is called an opposition. Opposition, as the word implies, tends to be challenging and requires some inner work to create harmony between the opposites.

At the Full Moon, you may feel the tension between the Sun and Moon as you're in the midst of it. It's a high-energy time of the month. It may be hard to sleep because of the bright light of the Moon and the heightened energy and intensity of the Full Moon time.

The Full Moon is a culminating time bringing plans, ideas, and projects to their fullness and fruition. This is why I encourage you to look at your results at this stage of the Moon cycle. The Full Moon may bring you clarity and insight. Harvest its illumination! As it's a culminating time, it's the perfect time to evaluate and assess your results.

In 2020, there was a very fertile New Moon in the summer in Cancer. There were very favorable aspects for seeding your

# The Magic Mirror

dreams on that particular Moon. I told Scott about it and encouraged him to put his big dreams into his New Moon wheel. He made a wheel and seeded his dream of building a house. He described the land and the elements very clearly. Two weeks later, on the Full Moon, he received a call about an opportunity to build a house on a beautiful piece of land in Sedona, AZ. He was surprised by what he wrote and what he received. In evaluating it in his Full Moon wheel, he realized he had manifested what he had asked for.

Another magic of the Full Moon is what I call 'The Magic Mirror.' With the heightened illumination of the Moon, this is the moment to catch a glimpse of the unconscious or subconscious patterns that are operating under the surface of your awareness. Invisible mechanisms can become visible to you.

To attune yourself to the Full Moon's energy, take time to self-reflect and pay attention to what's happening in your life. The Moon reflects the light of the Sun. The Sun represents your higher conscious awareness. The Moon represents the illusion of yourself—perhaps, the limited version you see and experience. As the Moon reflects the Sun, so must you utilize the reflected light of your higher self to see your subconscious self during this heightened time of seeing. You may see how you're connected to the Source and witness the source of your strength and immense power. You may also see the limitations, pain, suffering, and hidden emotional undercurrents directing and moving your life. The important part of the Full Moon is to be courageous and look in the magic mirror.

If you have a challenge you're facing repeatedly and are having difficulty figuring out what's going on, the Full Moon is the time to be open to receiving the necessary insights. I told you about the men I dated and how they didn't want intimacy. Then, one Full Moon, I saw it clear as day that it was me who was afraid of intimacy. Take the magic mirror and look honestly and deeply at yourself. Ask yourself why this situation keeps coming up and what you can change to transform the situation.

At the Full Moon, you're like a detective looking at the discrepancies between the clues. Some of the clues are your dreams and desires calling you forth. Other clues are what's happening in your life. Use your keen observational powers to evaluate your life and the difference between what you want and what's real. Observe where there's energy, enthusiasm, and action. Also, observe where the energy feels stale, where there's drudgery, and where there's avoidance. These are very helpful clues in creating the life of your dreams.

Important note: Be a dispassionate observer, like an anthropologist in a foreign land. There's no need to judge yourself or blame yourself. Rather, be honest, compassionate, and courageous to allow yourself to see what's happening and change it for the better.

The Full Moon part of the process is about consciously working with your karma. You can change your karma, as you can change your past, present, and future by addressing the truth of what's going on. To do this means having a desire and a commitment to take yourself on, as well as being as honest as possible with yourself. You're a Light Warrior! You've got this.

## How to Create a Full Moon Wheel:

For the Full Moon Wheel, you're going to make another Medicine Wheel. For this wheel, however, you're going to record your

# The Magic Mirror

observations and insights. This Moon Wheel is a self-portrait of what is and a map of your results.

### Full Moon: Observation & Self-Reflection

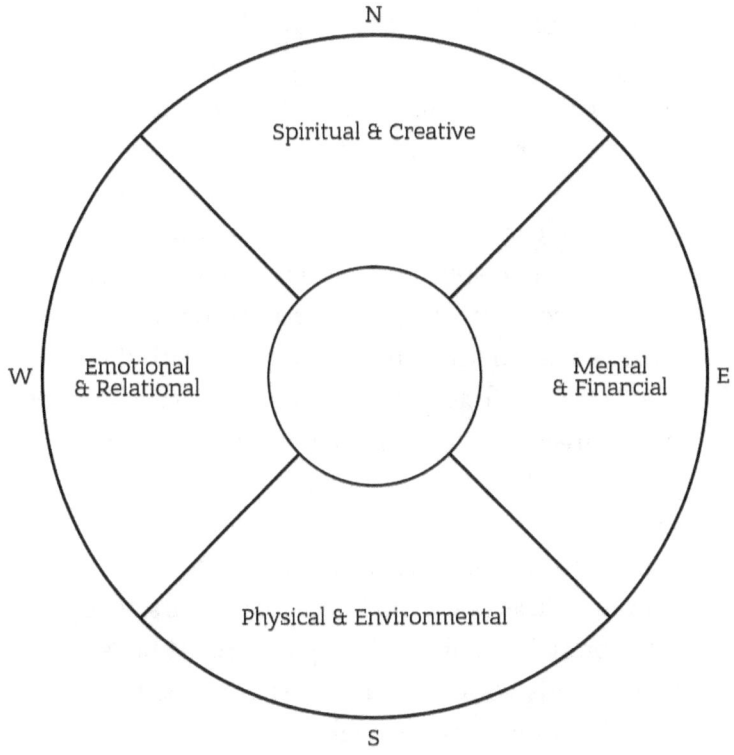

**Supplies:**
**11 x 14 paper**
**Pencil**
**Compass or large circle to trace**
**Ruler**
**Paint, markers, colored pencils, or other fun art supplies**

## Activating Lunar Alchemy

Making a Full Moon wheel:

1. Give yourself some time to get quiet and meditative to do your Full Moon Wheel.
2. Draw a Full Moon wheel, refer to the diagram.
3. If possible, create your Full Moon Wheel at the Full Moon or on the day of the Full Moon. The Full Moon energy is experienced the day before, the day of, and the day after the Full Moon, so sometimes, I record my insights over the course of several days.
4. Light a candle and ask for illumination and insight.
5. Consider each area of your life—mental, physical, emotional, and spiritual—and record your observations.
6. Look at your most recent New Moon Wheel and see what you asked for. What's happening with these 'seeds'?
7. Look at your life as a dispassionate observer. Be accepting of the insights and non-judgmental of yourself. Hold yourself in love as you look at what's really happening in your life.
8. This is an opportunity to see and record the results of your life. Be as open and honest with yourself as possible.
9. Ask yourself the following questions: What's working? What needs your attention? What needs to be healed? What's coming up for you?
10. Make it special: use paint, colored pencils, pens, glitter, or collage.

Your results are a mirror of you, both conscious and subconscious. If you're making progress and growth on a dream, you'll see it by recording this in your Full Moon Wheel. If you're not achieving what you desire, ask yourself why. See if your results give you clues to what's going on.

# The Magic Mirror

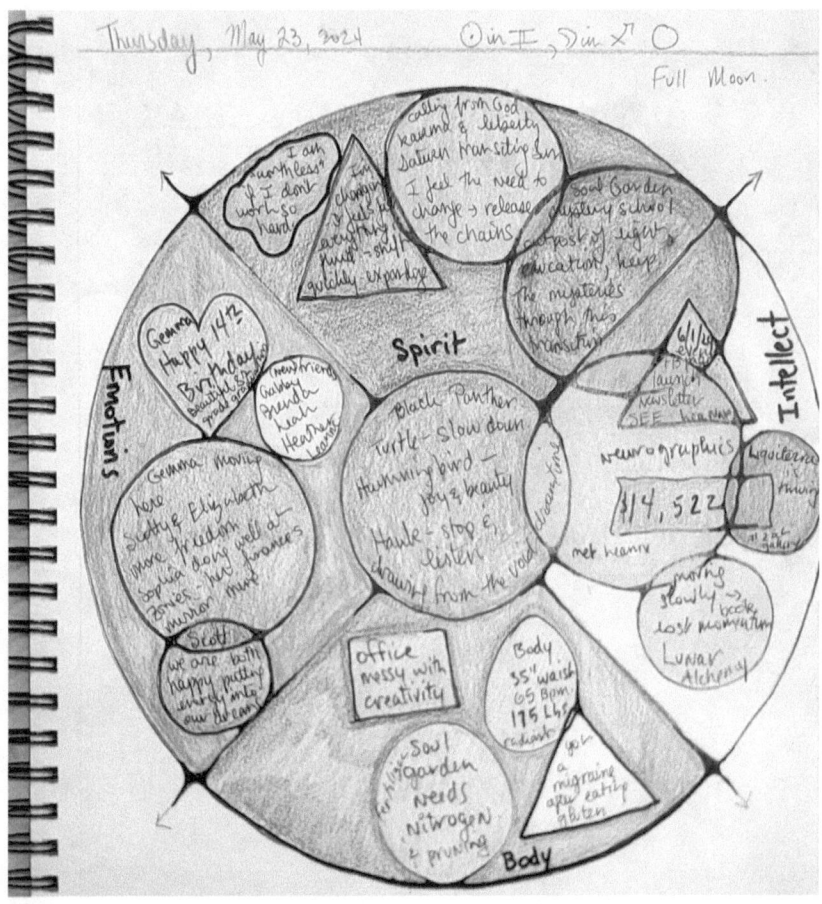

It's important that you want something—the dreams and desires you seeded in your New Moon Wheel. Wanting something will give you the longing to see what's going on and gain the necessary motivation to change if needed. For example, when I realized I wanted to get ordained and was seeding the energy of this dream month after month, I was looking for where the energy flow was happening, where I was making progress, and where I might have been stuck or had resistance. This is such valuable information because it tells you where to put more energy (behind the easy flow) and where to change or let go of old ways of doing things (the resistance).

**ACTIONS YOU CAN TAKE AS A RESULT OF READING THIS CHAPTER:**

1. Embrace the quiet self-reflection of the Full Moon to know thyself.

2. Be honest with yourself and observe what's happening.

3. Make a Full Moon Wheel to record your insights and self-reflection.

# CHAPTER 10

# The Magic of Transmutation

*"I am not what happened to me,
I am what I choose to become." – Carl Jung*

*"Once you realize you deserve a bright future,
letting go of your dark past is the best choice you will
ever make." – Roy T. Bennett*

*"Letting go may sound so simple, but rarely is it a one-time thing. Just keep letting go, until one day it's gone
for good." – Eleanor Brown*

# Activating Lunar Alchemy

This is where the magic happens! The Last Quarter Moon contains the secrets of alchemy and how to transmute your metaphorical lead into gold.

Every step of the Moon cycle is important. To experience the wholeness and healing of it, do each of the four steps of the Moon work and repeat. This last step of Lunar Alchemy sums up the alchemical workings of this process.

At the Last Quarter Moon, you attune yourself to the shedding and releasing of energy of the waning Moon. This has many benefits, especially in that this step is the key to transmuting your pain into abundance:

The benefits of shedding with the Last Quarter Moon are:

- Make space to receive spiritual abundance
- Letting go equals liberation
- Release your obstacles and move forward more easily
- Increase your inner peace and comfort
- Become unstoppable

Learning to let go has been difficult for me. My dad died when I was 10, and I wanted desperately to hold on to him. I also held onto the pain, loss, guilt, and grief. When I was growing up, these painful emotions snowballed into greater pain and suffering. Finally, the pain became too much to bear, and I had to start the process of letting go in order to unburden myself of the pain and move forward with my life.

### *Make space to receive spiritual abundance*
Part of the magic of this Moon work is in transmuting your darkness and shadow—your pain and suffering—into light,

# The Magic of Transmutation

healing, abundance, and pleasure. This transmutation process happens after the Full Moon, when you've seen and become aware of the patterns that aren't in harmony with what you want in your life. The Full Moon insights inform you of what to forgive and let go. When you make the decision to heal and change those limiting patterns, you free yourself to experience a new state of healing and abundance. As you continue to practice this work, your spiritual abundance increases as you let go of old habits, patterns, and behaviors.

## *Letting go equals liberation*
Being incarnated on Earth is limiting. You have the limitations of your human body, gravity, society, cultural beliefs, the constructs of knowledge, and your formative experiences. Yet, paradoxically, I believe you have everything you need to achieve your dreams. Anything is possible if you decide to achieve it and do the work.

Much of this work focuses on identifying and letting go of obstacles. Letting go of the limitations in your body, mind, emotions, and spirit liberates you to manifest your dreams. You experience limitations in your body such as sickness, disease, and pain. In your mind, you experience mental constructs, stories you tell yourself, false beliefs that you grew up with, and other limiting narratives. You experience a range of painful emotions, such as fear, shame, grief, and anger. In your spirit, you suffer from feeling disconnected from God and Spirit; in addition, you suffer and are in existential pain when you don't see yourself as worthy. As you work to let go of this type of pain and suffering, you become increasingly liberated and blessed.

## *Release your obstacles and move forward more easily.*
Recently, I have had debilitating back pain. It was my body's way of slowing me down and showing me how I was treating

myself. The back pain was literally an obstacle that immobilized me. I couldn't move forward because I couldn't move at all. As I became present with this pain and sought solutions for releasing it, I found that my back pain mirrored a deep fear of insecurity. To release the pain, I had some deep tissue healing work done on my back and body; I also looked inward to determine where I was emotionally and what I was feeling. Both the physical pain and the emotional pain—or fear—were holding me back. Once I began to acknowledge and address these obstacles and decided to let them go, I began to move forward again and experienced a profound healing.

### *Increase your inner peace and comfort*

I watched a video with Dagoba Priest Maledoma Somé. He explained that blessing is a state of the soul in which the psyche sits in comfort. If you're seeking inner peace and comfort, working on letting go of your pain and suffering on all levels of your being is one way of achieving this end. This Moon work is a process of letting go and stripping away to make way for more ease, peace, and comfort.

### *Become unstoppable*

Learning to navigate, move past, and let go of obstacles allows you to become unstoppable in pursuing your dreams. As I ask for and aspire for more, new challenges and obstacles come up for me. Sometimes, it's as simple as learning a new skill. At other times, the obstacle can be debilitating, like my back pain story above. When you let go and heal a challenge or obstacle, you increase your belief and ability to work through every subsequent obstacle. This is the magic of becoming unstoppable: knowing that as you grow, you'll face new challenges, know how to release them, and work through them to keep moving forward.

The Magic of Transmutation

## What is the Magic of the Last Quarter Moon?

At the Last Quarter Moon, the Moon is waning or getting smaller. You'll see the Last Quarter Moon in the morning sky above your head at sunrise. The Last Quarter will be illuminated on the left-hand side of the Moon and dark on the right. In astrology, the Last Quarter Moon makes a closing square to the Sun. This is an active energy and signifies that it's time to do the releasing work and psychological processing of the Moon cycle.

The energy of the Moon in the Last Quarter is shedding and getting smaller, and that energy is running out and getting less organized. It's like the tide is going out. To attune to the Moon's energy, you release and let go.

The magic of the Last Quarter is that it invites you into the alchemical process of transmutation, which changes a substance from one state to a superior state. The conservation of energy law states that matter is neither created nor destroyed in a closed system. Yet, it can be changed from one form to another. Working with the Moon will reveal the magic of how to do this.

When I let go during the Last Quarter Moon ritual, I'm making a choice and a decision to change the energy I'm experiencing physically, mentally, emotionally, or spiritually. Take the back pain story, for example; the guy who did my deep tissue bodywork didn't remove my back or my muscles. He took the stuck energy and transmuted it into ease and movement.

If you have a fear and decide to confront it, address it, and release it, you may be able to take that fear and turn it into courage, strength, or faith. This is transmutation as far as the human mechanism is concerned. You're taking one energy that appears to be blocking you and turning it into another energy that appears to be supporting you.

Letting go creates a vacuum. That vacuum will want to be filled up. So don't stop at letting go—fill yourself back up with what you dream and desire. Shortly after the Last Quarter releasing ritual, you'll be doing the New Moon ritual of 'seeding your dreams' again. This Moon work is the process of working with the continual rhythm of the Moon Cycle to build energy toward what you want and release what comes up that's holding you back. Profound healing change is possible.

As I have shared in my stories, letting go might feel difficult. Letting go could look like surrendering to God or Spirit and asking for Divine help. Letting go could also mean doing forgiveness work on yourself or with other people in your life. Letting go could also mean 'grieving'.

There's a saying, "Life is for me." When I began to embrace this saying a few years ago, I began to look at all my troubles, pains, limitations, and obstacles as opportunities for growth. As I've increasingly embraced this idea, I've come to the realization that I could be grateful for these difficulties. Being grateful for these challenges opens me up to see how life is for me and how to transmute my pain into spiritual abundance.

# The Magic of Transmutation

## How to make a Last Quarter wheel

At the New Moon, you seeded your dreams. Then, you took supportive action in the First Quarter. At the Full Moon, you looked in the magic mirror and assessed what was happening in your life. Now, it's time to shed with the Moon, release, and let go of anything that doesn't align with your dreams and desires.

If this were a garden, you planted seeds (New Moon), you watered and fertilized them (First Quarter), you observed the delicate sprouts coming up (Full Moon), and now it's time to weed, prune, or cut back anything that's threatening the growth of these seedlings.

The Last Quarter wheel has two halves like the First Quarter wheel. On the left side of your wheel, you're going to write what you want to create, your dreams, and your desires. Your dreams and desires may have shifted a bit after following the Moon cycle process. You may have more clarity and gained some valuable insights. Reconsider your dreams and desires as you make this Moon wheel.

Activating Lunar Alchemy

## Last Quarter: Releasing & Shedding

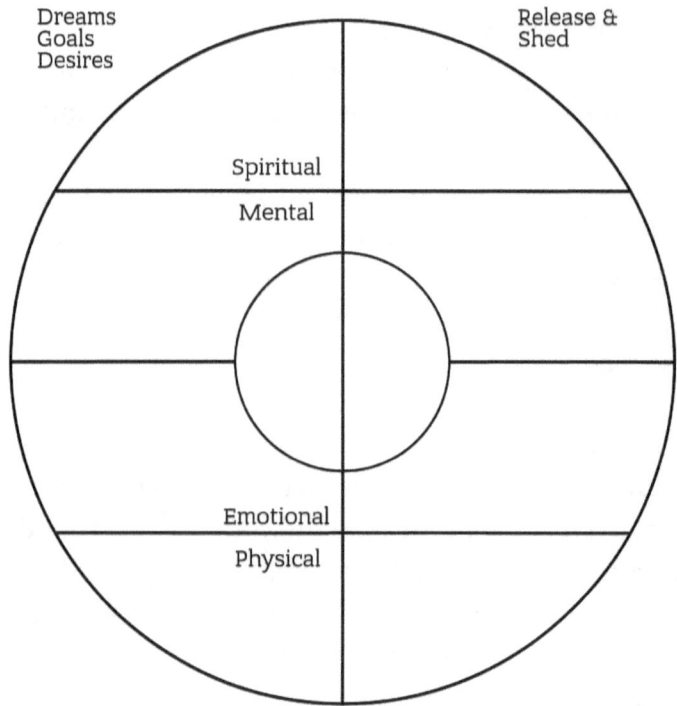

On the right side of the Moon Wheel, write what you want to release and let go of. You can release objects, behaviors, habits, lies, stories, or emotions. At the Full Moon, you gather increasing awareness about what's working and moving and what's holding you back. In the Last Quarter Wheel, you release what's holding you back.

Consider the different quadrants: physical, mental, emotional, and spiritual. Ask yourself, 'What do I want?' and 'What's holding me back?' in each of these areas. For example, dairy gives me sinus congestion. If I want to reduce or release dairy, I time it

# The Magic of Transmutation

with the Moon Cycle. I write, 'I want clear sinuses' on the left side of the wheel and, 'I easily release dairy' on the right side of the wheel.

Take time for gratitude. This Last Quarter process works best for me when I'm grateful for where I am, what has happened in the past to get me here, and where I'm going. The beliefs, behaviors, emotions, or objects you're releasing have helped you get to this point. Giving thanks for the things you're letting go of is very powerful and will change your relationship with those challenges.

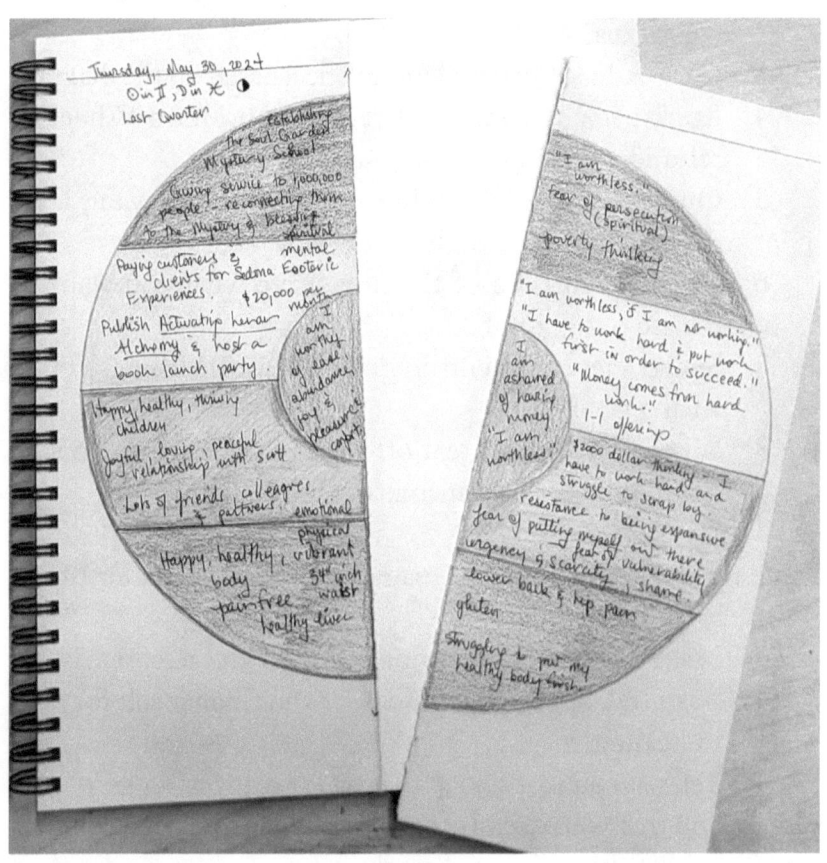

# Activating Lunar Alchemy

Creating the Last Quarter Moon Wheel:

**Supplies:**
**11 x 14 paper**
**Compass or large circle to trace**
**Ruler**
**Paint, markers, colored pencils, or other fun art supplies**
**Scissors**
**Lighter or matches**

1. Make some sacred space and time for yourself.
2. Make it special, light a candle, or get a glass of wine or cup of tea
3. Create a Last Quarter Moon Wheel based on the diagram
4. Look back at your most recent Full Moon Wheel to remind yourself of your insights
5. On the left side of the line, write what you want, your dreams, and your desires
6. On the right side of the line, write what you want to release or let go of
7. Spend a few moments in gratitude for the things you're letting go of
8. When you're done, tear off the right side and burn it as a symbolic act of transmuting it into light.

Some tips for supporting the magic of this Last Quarter ritual:

➢ Make a conscious decision to let go and release.
➢ Ask God, Spirit, your guides, or your higher self for help in healing.
➢ Tell your subconscious that you're ready to let go of this and that you're ready to receive whatever is on the other side of this pain or obstacle.

# The Magic of Transmutation

You may have circumstances in your life that seem like impossible limitations or situations that you need external help with. The Moon work has its limitations, too. In some cases, you'll need other support; for example, in my back pain story, I did the self-care of the Moon work, and I also went to a professional to help me deal with the back pain. I engaged in other healing modalities and sought other healers to help me work through the debilitating feelings I was experiencing in my life. That process took me weeks to work through.

## What if I have mental and emotional blocks?

Mental and emotional blocks are tricky. They seduce you into believing they're real. What you believe about yourself is compelling and seems very real, and the emotions you feel can have a powerful influence on you.

A mental block, debilitating emotions, or limiting beliefs are in your psyche and energy field. They can be a construct of your thinking that's attempting to protect you from something. These blocks can be informed by life experiences, things you were taught as a child, societal beliefs, and more. In my experience, limiting beliefs and emotions are attempting to protect you from feeling some hidden emotion, maybe even protect you from remembering or reliving a traumatic experience.

For the longest time in my life, I behaved and acted as if I was unworthy. In my 20s and 30s, I struggled to make more than $10,000 a year (even though I was highly educated and skilled!). I didn't believe or act like I deserved money. I didn't see that I had value to give.

## Activating Lunar Alchemy

In addition, I didn't apply to the Crucible program for over 20 years to let myself go through the education to get ordained because I didn't feel worthy to serve God. Even in my relationships, I treated myself like a second-class citizen, putting everyone else's needs first, focusing my energy on rescuing others, and not considering what I wanted or needed.

Feeling unworthy kept me from giving, being authentic, and living a meaningful life. I finally decided to confront this unworthiness, challenge it, and cut it off. The limiting belief that I was unworthy was hiding and protecting me from a deep sense of shame. With this Moon work, I realized that I had a deep shame about asking for what I wanted and also asking for money for my work.

Although it has taken me a while to work through the layers, I've repeatedly released the belief that I'm unworthy in my Last Quarter Moon rituals. I've also released the shame behind it, allowing me to put my focus back on what I want to create. As a result, I have begun to realize the value I have to give.

Can you see the magic of this part of the Moon Cycle? Your limiting beliefs, painful emotions, unwanted behaviors, bad habits, challenges and obstructions can be let go of, loved and accepted. This frees your energy to be put toward your purposeful endeavors.

This Last Quarter Moon work could be easily overlooked, especially if you have a hard time letting go. Yet, this is a very important part of the creative magic of the Moon work.

## The Magic of Transmutation

**ACTIONS YOU CAN TAKE AS A RESULT OF READING THIS CHAPTER:**

1. Let go of patterns, behaviors, or habits that no longer serve you.

2. Create your Last Quarter Moon Wheel.

3. Practice gratitude for the hard circumstances, challenges, and pains.

# CHAPTER 11

# The Magic of Attention

*"This is the first, wildest, and wisest thing I know, that the soul exists, and that it is built entirely out of attention." – Mary Oliver*

*"The moment one gives close attention to anything, even a blade of grass, it becomes a mysterious, awesome, indescribably magnificent world in itself."*
*– Henry Miller*

# Activating Lunar Alchemy

Attention is one of the most powerful manifesting tools that you have access to.

*Where your attention goes, energy flows.* As I've learned to schedule, commit, and command my attention, my life has truly transformed into one of meaning, purpose, joy and even abundance. One reason this has happened is because I have focused my attention on what I wanted to bring forth in my life, and my life has changed to reflect that attention.

Here are a few of the benefits of learning to direct and govern your attention:

- Attention brings higher performance
- Attention stimulates engagement, and engagement brings you joy
- Attention is the medium for which thoughts become things
- Controlling or focusing your attention is one key to transforming your life
- Attention tells your mind what to encode in memory; therefore, your memories reflect the focus of your attention

### *Attention brings higher performance*
Sustained attention is a type of attention that allows you to concentrate deeply on a task for a specified period of time. This type of attention can help you accomplish complex tasks. If you're attempting to create anything, periods of sustained attention will propel you forward on a given project.

For example, my husband and I started an art business in 2019. I spent over six months doing short, one- to two-hour bursts of sustained attention each day to build the infrastructure of the business and create the marketing and sales system. I utilized my sustained attention on different tasks depending on the steps of the project. In the beginning, I used my attention to do business classes, such as taking a three-month business training program and then implementing the steps. Later in the process, my sustained attention was focused on organic marketing. At other times, my sustained attention was on ideation and creating new art pieces. Now, my attention is on producing art for sale and keeping the sales system going.

When we started the business, I was doing it part-time and working another job. Now, the business supports my husband and I full-time.

### *Attention stimulates engagement, engagement brings you joy*
Do you allow yourself to get fully absorbed in a task? Once you're fully absorbed and giving your full attention, you're most likely enjoying what you're doing. You feel stimulated and alive. You may also feel productive and joyful. One of the psychological aspects of attention is that it brings you into full engagement with what you're doing.

### *Attention is the medium for which thoughts become things*
You may have heard the saying, "Thoughts become things." However, I think it takes more than thoughts to bring something forth. Focusing your attention and directing it on those thoughts allows them to become things because where your attention goes, energy flows, and thoughts need energy to become real, tangible, and manifest.

## Activating Lunar Alchemy

When creating something, whether it's a business or an art piece, you're extending your energy outward with attention. This is a form of engagement, and engagement puts you in a relationship with the concept or object you're working with. On the one hand, this is a psychological process, controlled by the executive function of the brain. Yet, at a deeper level, this is an energetic process of focusing your energy on manipulating the environment around you. Do you realize how powerful this is? You control your attention, and that controls the flow of energy. If used consistently and appropriately, any complex idea can be brought to reality with the right application of attention.

### *Controlling or focusing your attention is a key to transforming your life*

I'm good at scheduling and directing my attention. I use this skill for writing, problem-solving, creating art, building my business, and pretty much everything I'm working to accomplish.

With the process of Lunar Alchemy, you're directing your attention to attuning to the Moon cycle to create change, healing, and transformation in your life. At the New Moon, you're focusing your attention on listening to your higher self to determine what you want to create in your life. This is a receptive form of attention. In the First Quarter, you're focusing your attention on supportive actions toward what you want to create. On the Full Moon, you're commanding your attention to focus on self-reflection so you can evaluate your life and what's happening around you. This allows you to see yourself and get insights into what's going on in your subconscious. At the Last Quarter Moon, you're focusing your attention and energy on releasing what isn't working for you.

# The Magic of Attention

As you continue to follow this cycle, your energy focuses on what you want to create in your life and as a result of putting your energy there consistently, your life begins to reflect this attention and energy.

***Attention tells your mind what to encode in memory; therefore, your memories reflect the focus of your attention***
A couple of years ago, I heard a fascinating news story on NPR. In the long run of your life, what you remember and what's meaningful to you is based on where you put your attention. Where you put your attention signifies to your mind and energy field what's important to you. When possible, focus on what you value and care about. *Align your attention with your intention!*

At the end of your life, I want your memories to be happy ones of living your dreams and fulfilling your bucket list. If you're putting your valuable attention into tasks you dislike or dread, you need to stop that as soon as possible. If you put your energy into what you dread, you create more of that for yourself.

## What is Attention?

According to author Grace Lindsay, who wrote *Attention in Psychology, Neuroscience, and Machine Learning*, "Attention is the important ability to flexibly control limited computational resources."[14]

There are different types of attention, including the following:

> ➢ Focused attention is when your attention is drawn to an external stimulus so you can quickly attend to the stimulus.

## Activating Lunar Alchemy

> - Alternating attention requires you to stop one task, tend to another, and then resume the original task.
> - Limited attention is doing two or more things at once, like driving and listening to Audible, also known as multitasking. According to psychological studies, multitasking isn't a very effective form of attention.
> - Selective attention is when you tune out external stimuli to focus your attention on one specific task. Selective attention is a miracle and shows both how amazing the brain is and the limitations of its functioning.
> - Sustained attention is when you pick a task and focus solely on it for a prescribed period.

"Attention can reasonably be thought of as the output of executive control."[15] It takes a lot of energy to run the executive control center of your brain. "The human brain can focus for up to two hours, but it needs a 20-to-30-minute break after that."[16]

This is important to note because "Attention is a limited resource."[17] So, you want to be deliberate about how you use your attention. Attention is limited in terms of the brain's computational capacity, thinking, focus, working memory, the number of demands on the brain, and the amount of energy running the executive function demands.

Another consideration is about your biorhythm and determining the best time for you to put your attention on your goals and dreams. "Studies reveal that 90% of people do their best thinking outside of the office early in the morning or late at night."[18] Be strategic with your attention and direct it to what matters most to you.

# The Magic of Attention

For example, the easiest time for me to focus and sustain my attention is in the morning. I plan my schedule and routine around focusing between 8 am and 12 pm. I have another peak between 2 pm and 4 pm. As the day goes on, my ability to pay attention diminishes. Usually, by 6 pm, I'm not able to give attention to complex and demanding mental tasks. I prioritize what I want to accomplish around the peaks in my mental clarity.

## Your Attention Budget

Your attention is precious and a limited resource, so it's advantageous to be deliberate and strategic with it. Attention isn't solely about the quantity of time you invest. It's more about the quality of your attention. It can be as simple as meditation, prayer, or even a few focused minutes on what you want to create. The key is consistently putting your attention where it matters and releasing distractions that hinder your progress.

My husband, Scott, and I developed the Attention Budget to help ourselves focus our creative energy amid our busy, hectic lives. The Attention Budget tool was inspired by YNAB (You Need a Budget) founder Jesse Mecham, who says, "Scarcity brings clarity." Similar to creating a financial budget to manage and be deliberate about your financial resources, the Attention Budget helps you manage and be deliberate about your attention and focus.

## Attention Budget

Top Values & Priorities:

1.

2.

3.

4.

5.

| Mon | Tue | Wed | Thu | Fri | Sat | Sun |
|-----|-----|-----|-----|-----|-----|-----|
|     |     |     |     |     |     |     |
|     |     |     |     |     |     |     |
|     |     |     |     |     |     |     |
|     |     |     |     |     |     |     |

# The Magic of Attention

I was an elementary school teacher when we came up with this tool. I enjoyed the job and found it very rewarding, but I was working seven days a week (prepping on weekends), and all of my creative energy and attention was going into my teaching job. As I continued my Lunar Alchemy work, I found that what I wanted to create was in increasing misalignment with what I was spending my attention on.

One of my dreams and desires was to develop and teach this Moon work. As most of my attention and energy was focused on my teaching job, I didn't have a lot of extra attention, energy, or time to develop my Moon business.

As I used the Attention Budget tool alongside my Moon wheels, I began being very deliberate about where I put my attention, focus, and extra time in alignment with my dreams, desires, and goals. I put my Moon work and business work in my Attention Budget as the first square in the morning before going to school. Gradually, the Moon work began to build. I started teaching classes and scheduling sessions to teach the work.

I also used the Attention Budget to focus more on my kids and my relationship with Scott. As a result, my life shifted, and my relationships improved, reflecting where I put my attention.

Using this Attention Budget demonstrated to me that where your attention goes, energy flows, and being deliberate with my attention helped me manifest my dreams and desires faster.

The Attention Budget is an optional tool to use with the Moon Wheels. However, if you're in a transition or very busy juggling multiple demands, the Attention Budget is a valuable tool for managing your attention (and limited time) regarding your dreams and desires.

The Attention Budget is a table broken down into the seven days of the week, with four blocks of time each day. This isn't meant to be used like a planner, diary, or scheduling tool. The blocks don't represent a fixed amount of time; rather, they represent an area of focused attention. There are 28 attention squares in the week. Your job in filling out this attention budget is to decide how to allocate your attention among these 28 squares.

On a given day, we have a finite amount of attention. For the sake of this practice, you divide your attention into four key areas each day, where you direct your attention, spend your time, and give your energy in these areas.

Use your top values and priorities to guide your choices and organize your Attention Budget. Draw from your New Moon Wheel, looking at your dreams and desires to figure out where to put your attention. Whether it's your family, business, health, or spiritual journey, these are the seeds of your dreams. Nurture them with your attention and place them in your Attention Budget.

It's essential to keep your Attention Budget manageable, typically focusing on four or five core priorities per week. Less is often more when it comes to effective attention allocation. When I'm at my most productive, I'm concentrating on just a few critical priorities. I've learned that slowing down and dedicating attention to a single task can produce greater accomplishments and quicker success.

# The Magic of Attention

Attention Budget  Nov. 20 - 26, 2023

Top Values & Priorities:

1. Finish writing my book (Book)

2. Exercise (Ex)

3. Family time (FT)

4. Holiday Art Sale

5.

| Mon | Tue | Wed | Thu | Fri | Sat | Sun |
|---|---|---|---|---|---|---|
| Ex | Ex | Ex | Ex | Ex | Ex | Ex |
| Book | Book | Book | Book | Art Sale | Art Sale | FT |
| Class Prep | Book | Art Sale | Art Sale | Art Sale | Art Sale | FT |
| Monday Class | FT | FT | FT | FT | FT | FT |

# Activating Lunar Alchemy

Model your own Attention Budget from my example:

1. Put the dates of the week at the top of the page.
2. Underneath the date, define your top priorities for the week. Refer to your most recent New Moon Wheel to determine where you would like to *align your attention with your intentions*. For example, right now, my top priority is finishing my book. I'm going to make sure that I allocate time and attention to completing it.
3. My second priority is exercise and maintaining my health to support getting sleep and feeling good enough to concentrate when I'm writing. Exercise helps me relieve stress, reduces my anxious mental state, and gets me out of my head. Exercise also helps me restore my inner calm and grounding.
4. My next priority is spending quality time with my family. This usually entails making dinner and often playing a game afterward.
5. My last priority is the holiday art sales I have coming up this weekend. Although this is where I make my income, my top attention priority is my book.
6. When I have prior commitments and obligations, I block those squares out first. This allows me to see what time is remaining to allocate my attention. This week, the holiday art sales on Thursday, Friday, and Saturday constitute a prior commitment.
7. After I have blocked out the squares for the week, I color code them using colored pencils to quickly refer to where I want to put my attention.
8. Follow your Attention Budget as best you can throughout the week.

## The Magic of Attention

To get extra benefits from this Attention Budget, track how you spent your attention at the end of the week. Did you follow your Attention Budget, or did you end up attending to other activities? Tracking will give you valuable information about yourself, your attention, and where you spend your time and energy. Tracking will ultimately lead you to make positive changes for yourself.

### ACTIONS YOU CAN TAKE AS A RESULT OF READING THIS CHAPTER:

1. Determine your top three to five priorities for the week by looking at your New Moon and First Quarter Moon wheels.

2. Fill out the Attention Budget and schedule several blocks of sustained attention around your dreams and desires.

3. At the end of the week, track what happened. Did you put attention into your dreams? What was the result?

# CHAPTER 12

# The Magic of Listening

"Listen to your own voice, your own soul; too many people listen to the noise of the world instead of themselves." – Leon Brown

"At the center of your being you have the answer; you know who you are, and you know what you want."
– Lao Tzu

"The Universe is not outside of you. Look inside yourself; everything that you want, you already are."
– Rumi

# Activating Lunar Alchemy

There's so much going on in the world and your hectic modern life that it's easy not to pay attention or listen to yourself. Yet, the answers come from within; listening is the magic of tuning inward.

There are many benefits of taking time to tune inward and listen to yourself, including:

- Listening is receptive and develops inner peace and happiness
- Listening promotes connection with your higher self
- Listening increases your self-awareness
- Listening develops your intuition
- Listening and responding establishes trust in yourself and authenticity

As a 20-something, I had so much noise and chatter in my psyche that I couldn't perceive what I felt, wanted, or needed. I was in a lot of emotional pain. My thoughts were filled with a lot of negative self-talk. When I began to tune into myself and listen to my body, intellect, emotions, and spirit, I began to feel a lot better, and I found ways to heal and grow.

For example, I had been raped twice in my teens. I didn't really stop to listen to the mental-emotional anguish going on inside of me until I started doing self-portrait paintings in my 20s. Then, I started paying attention to what I was feeling and began listening to my body and feelings and what they were communicating.

At first, it took a lot of effort to sink into this time of listening to myself. However, with practice, I began to develop the skill of listening to my body, mind, emotions, and spirit. In turn, the skill of listening has developed my intuition, empathy, and sensitivity to myself and others.

In my case, after the rapes, the loss of my dad, and the other painful stuff I had endured, I don't think I wanted to hear, see, or feel how I was feeling or what was really going on with me. Rather, I had tuned myself out in order to cope. There was plenty of noise and distraction to drown my pain out and ignore what was really going on with me.

### *Listening is receptive and develops inner peace and happiness*

As I began to pay attention and listen to my body, emotions, thoughts, and spiritual callings, I began to be able to respond to my needs and desires. Gradually, as I began to listen and respond to my inner self, my sense of inner peace expanded because my psyche wasn't crying out so loudly to get my attention. I learned ways to soothe myself and work through emotional pain. I also found that I knew what I wanted and needed and could take action to make that a reality for myself.

### *Listening promotes connection with your higher self*

I've always been interested in journaling and writing. In my late 20s, I learned about 'morning pages' from *The Artist's Way* by Julia Cameron. Morning Pages are a discipline of sitting and handwriting three pages from your stream of consciousness each morning. At first, you might not know what to write. Then, you start writing about how you feel and what's going on in your life. As you peel away the layers through this writing, you tap into a deeper sense of self and creativity.

After doing the morning pages for several weeks, I began to feel present with myself. I knew how I felt and what was going on with me. Then, I started to develop a relationship with my higher self and creativity. It's like I wrote through all of the crap that cluttered the surface of my mind and broke through to the other side. By listening and tuning inward consistently, you're able to get past the monkey mind and emotional noise that's keeping you from hearing your higher self and your guidance.

### *Listening gives you greater self-awareness*
When you listen to your body, you develop a sense of awareness of how you feel, what you need, and what your body is telling you. You can also listen to your thoughts and what you say, this will tell you a lot about what you think and believe about yourself. You can listen to your emotions and find out how you're feeling. You can also listen to your spirit and receive inner guidance. These different types of listening to yourself all require you to tune your focus inward. Like tuning into a radio station, you're tuning into a specific part of yourself. All of this gives you greater self-awareness.

About eight years ago, when I realized I wanted to do my spiritual work professionally, I kept hearing my inner critic say, "You're crazy."

This thought, playing over and over in my head, was a giant mental block keeping me from putting myself out there. I spent quite a while letting go of and removing this damaging thought pattern from my mind. The amazing thing is this negative self-talk was happening for years before I heard it.

### *Listening develops your intuition*
Tuning inward and listening will help you develop your intuition. As you develop listening and feeling in your body, you'll also start to hear your gut instincts talking to you. Similarly, as you

begin to listen to your thoughts and emotions, you'll also start to develop your intuition. I would say your intuition is already there; you just need to tune into it. You may also receive thoughts about situations and other people. This is valuable intuitive information you're tuning into.

### *Listening and responding establishes trust in yourself and authenticity*

It's one thing to hear and then do nothing. Listening is about hearing what's happening and then responding appropriately. As you develop your inner listening and respond to it, you'll start to trust yourself, your body, emotions, gut, and intuition. Learning to trust yourself, what you want, and what to do about it is crucial for feeling empowered and authentic.

I spent many years rejecting my intuition and feeling frustrated. I would have a fleeting thought and ignore it. Then, I would regret not listening to it. Often, I knew what to do, yet didn't do it. As I began to listen to these fleeting thoughts and respond appropriately, my outcomes positively increased. My life has improved and become more enjoyable since I started listening to and following my intuition.

## What is the Magic of Listening?

Listening isn't just about hearing; it's also about responding appropriately. According to the etymological definition of the verb, *to listen*, listening means 'to hear and attend to': 'Old English *hlysnan* (Northumbrian *lysna*) 'to listen, hear; attend to, obey.'[19]

This is a critically important distinction in listening versus hearing; you don't just hear it, but you listen for it and attend to it. This goes back to my example about my intuition; I heard my intuition for several years and didn't attend to it. I wasn't really *listening*.

In December 1992, I was working on my senior thesis at college before the end of the semester. I had a lot of work to do, and I planned to work on campus and go to the library. That afternoon, I suddenly had an impulse to go home. I knew I needed to be studying and working, but I felt a strong pull to go home. So, I listened and went. Later that night, I got a hysterical call from a friend that there had been a mass shooting on my college campus, and some of my friends and professors were killed in the library. This was a horrific and life-changing event. I was safe at home because I listened to this impulse. I feel so lucky and grateful to have been warned and to have listened to my intuition.

You'll naturally develop your intuition as you listen to your body, emotions, thoughts, and spirit. By listening to these aspects of yourself, you're becoming consciously aware of what has remained in your subconscious awareness. Your intuition is information available to you through sensing, hearing, or seeing. If you're not listening to yourself, you may not be tuned into your intuition.

Listening is a receptive action. Sometimes, it's difficult to listen if your mind is filled with thoughts and chatter. If I have a lot going on in my mind when I want to settle down and listen, I write a list or get those thoughts down on paper so I can clear my mind to receive.

Listening is an important part of *this Moon work*. You listen at the New Moon in order to seed your dreams and define what you want. You listen for supportive actions at the First Quarter Moon that will help nurture your seeds. You tune inward and

## The Magic of Listening

self-reflect at the Full Moon to evaluate what's happening with your seeds and reveal what's happening in your subconscious. Then, in the Last Quarter Moon, you listen for what you want to keep and what's holding you back, and then you cut away the habits, beliefs, emotions, and behaviors that no longer serve you.

## How to apply listening to Lunar Alchemy

At the New Moon, I recommend that you *listen*. You must listen to yourself to know your dreams and desires and to put what you want in your New Moon Wheel. The New Moon is a particularly potent time to listen to your higher self, as your emotional self (Moon) and higher conscious self (Sun) are in alignment.

I highly recommend listening to yourself daily. Tune in deeply to what you want and need. This will greatly accelerate the success of your Moon work.

There are different ways to tune in and listen to yourself, such as journaling, doing art, meditation, morning pages, and prayer. Pick one that suits you. Listening requires you to slow down and pay attention to what's happening with yourself. Doing the Moon wheels weekly will help you develop the ability to turn inward and listen.

If you're seeking greater creativity and a sense of self, do 'Morning Pages' from Julia Cameron's *The Artist's Way*. This is a great practice for getting past the monkey mind and the emotional gunk to the deep reaches of yourself.

Another way that I like to tune into myself and listen is to do some simple sketching with my non-dominant hand. This technique allows you to tap into the emotional centers of your right brain, which are often overpowered by your left brain's well-developed analytical centers.

For this technique, I use my left hand because I'm right-handed. Here's a recent example: I was having some pain in my stomach area; it felt like my stomach was burning and also like I was very nervous. I touched my stomach with my dominant (right) hand and drew a sketch of what I was feeling with my non-dominant (left) hand. What I drew was a sloppy sketch of my inner child feeling scared and insecure. Then, using my non-dominant hand, I wrote out in short sentences what that feeling was telling me, such as, "I'm scared."

It turns out that I was feeling anxious about the financial situation I was dealing with at the time. This technique helped me quickly get to the essence of the matter because I engaged the emotional centers of my brain with my non-dominant hand and evaded my analytical mind.

Another method I use is asking myself a question and using it as a free writing prompt.

For example:
Question: Why does my stomach feel this way?
Answer: My stomach hurts because I'm feeling anxious. I'm scared and nervous.

This technique may take a little more writing and effort to get to the essence of the matter. You may even need to ask more questions. However, if you let yourself get into the flow, you'll often find that you have the answer you're seeking, or you'll come up with something surprising and brilliant.

## ACTIONS YOU CAN TAKE AS A RESULT OF READING THIS CHAPTER:

1. Make time to listen to yourself daily.

2. Respond to what you hear.

3. Practice one of the suggested listening practices.

# CHAPTER 13

# The Magic of Decision

*"Decision is a sharp knife that cuts clean and straight; indecision, a dull one that hacks and tears and leaves ragged edges behind it."* – Gordon Graham

*"Decision making is power. Most people don't have the guts to make a 'tough decisions' because they want to make the 'right decision' and so they make 'no decision'. Remember, life is short, so do things that matter the most and have the courage to make 'tough decisions' and to chase your dreams."* – Yama Mubtakeraker

# Activating Lunar Alchemy

*"When faced with a decision, choose the path that feeds your soul." – Dorothy Mendoza Row*

I've made a few big decisions that have changed the course of my life in a radical way. Once you decide to do something, even if it seems like an improbable task, you figure out a way to do it.

Your ability to choose what you want out of life is one of your most profound gifts. When you truly decide to do something, you open yourself to the possibilities and solutions of making it a reality. The benefits of the decision are many:

- Decision brings clarity
- Decision propels you to move forward
- Decision reveals what to say 'yes' to and what to say 'no' to
- Decision is the ultimate power to live the life you want to live—the secret to achievement
- Decision liberates your energy and focus

### *Decision brings clarity*
What if you don't know what you want in life? You could ask yourself what your purpose is, what your destiny is, and so forth, but you may never find clarity. When you *decide* to figure out what you want, you'll start moving in the right direction. As you move and take action to figure out what you want, you'll receive clarity.

### *Decision propels forward*
When you make a true decision, you suddenly have what you need to move forward and take action. The magic of decision is that it liberates you. In contrast, indecision keeps you stuck and circling.

# The Magic of Decision

## *Decision reveals what to say 'yes' to and what to say 'no' to*

When you know what you want and have decided to make it happen, you get very clear on what to say 'yes' to and what to say 'no' to. Your decision gives you the clarity to ask yourself, "Is this in alignment with what I have decided?" Yes or no? This kind of clarity helps you figure out what to do with your precious resources: your time, attention, desire, and creativity.

## *The ultimate power to live the life you want to live*

Knowing what you want and deciding to make it a reality gives you the ultimate power to live the life you want to live. I see two challenging steps to this. First, you need to figure out what you want and define your dream. Second, decide to make it a reality. If you've done this before in your life—figured out what you wanted, decided to do it, and did it—use this experience to bolster your self-belief. Know that what you want is possible and will give you meaning and purpose.

## *Decision liberates your energy and focus*

Decision involves making a choice between options, which implies that some options are cut off and no longer weigh you down. You can also use your magic of decision to get out of pain, not to live in scarcity, or heal from feeling abandoned. I've made all of these decisions and have been successful. Since I've decided to do meaningful work, pursue my dreams, and feel happy and healthy, by necessity, I've had to let go of my old way of doing things. This has liberated my energy and attention and directed me to what really matters.

In contrast, indecision keeps you stuck in limbo, where you're going in circles rather than moving toward your dreams. Indecision often comes from a fear of failure and a misperception about failure. What if you perceived a failure as data informing you on how to improve?

I worked on the Children with Incarcerated Parents Task Force for over three years. The task we were assigned was to conduct a study of children with incarcerated parents and give recommendations to the Coconino County Criminal Justice Coordinating Council. For the first few years, we were defining the situation and how to gather data about it. We tried and failed to get information several times. However, in the act of focusing on the outcome of providing these recommendations, we finally decided what the critical issues were and how to obtain some empirical data. There were a lot of failed attempts before we eventually succeeded.

## What is the Magic of Decision?

The root of the word *decide* literally means 'to cut off'.[20]

*late 14c., 'to settle a dispute, determine a controversy,' from Old French decider, from Latin decidere 'to decide, determine,' literally 'to cut off,' from de 'off' (see* **de-**) *+ caedere 'to cut' (from PIE root* **\*kae-id-** *'to strike'). For Latin vowel change, see* **acquisition**. *Sense is of resolving difficulties 'at a stroke.' Meaning 'to make up one's mind' is attested from 1830. Related:* **Decided**; *deciding.*

Deciding is magical in and of itself. When you decide, you take your God-given power to choose between what you want to keep and what you want to cut off. Deciding is one of the most powerful tools you possess to create what you want in your life. The magic of decision is in giving yourself only one option and then being moved to accomplish it. The moment you make a clear decision is a magical moment as you begin the transformative process toward your chosen outcome.

# The Magic of Decision

I've made a few decisions I wasn't sure I could accomplish. The one that sticks out in my mind was healing from my anxious attachment and getting into a secure and loving relationship. I made up my mind to do it, no matter what. This taught me that when you honestly decide to accomplish something, nothing can stop you from figuring it out.

## How do you wield the Magic of Decision?

Your life is like a garden. You get to choose what you want and how to cultivate it. In cultivating your garden, you use the magic of decision at every step of the process.

First, you must decide on what kind of garden you want. Where's it going to be planted? What do you want to grow? This is akin to deciding on your dream.

When you've decided to grow a garden, you may sketch it or make a garden bed (like making a Moon wheel). By taking action, you're deciding how to create the garden. Then, you might prepare the soil and get your garden bed ready for planting.

When your soil is ready, you plant your seeds. You choose these seeds, just like at the New Moon.

After you plant your seeds, you can decide whether to water and fertilize your garden, or you may decide just to ignore it. But if you've decided that you want to cultivate the garden of your dreams, you'll water and nurture your seeds, just like taking supportive action at the First Quarter Moon.

## Activating Lunar Alchemy

Then, your plants begin to grow, and you feel the satisfaction and pleasure of this process. You also notice that other plants are growing, too. Some of the plants are the ones you planted, and others are 'weeds' or non-deliberate plants. You observe this in the Full Moon phase. At this time, you could also decide whether to observe your garden or not.

As you observe the growing plants in your garden, you decide what to keep, what to cut back, and what to remove (Last Quarter Moon). You could also decide to plant more seeds.

You might notice that the weeds around the plants threaten to overtake them. What do you do? Do you leave the garden and let the non-deliberate plants take over? Or do you cut away the weeds and plants you don't want? When you make way for what you're deliberately growing, you're using your magic of decision to choose what you want to grow and put your resources into.

Deciding and cutting off gives you the freedom to choose what you want to create and how to focus your precious resources (mental, physical, emotional, or spiritual) toward that end.

## Applying Decision to Lunar Alchemy:

### *Decision and Pain*
This is a hard one for me to tell you. If you're in a lot of pain, physically, mentally, emotionally, or spiritually, decide to do whatever it takes to get out of pain and get into a state of comfort and blessing. I've been in a lot of pain in my life, some physical and spiritual and a lot of emotional pain. I've been on a healing journey because I decided that I didn't want to be in pain any longer.

# The Magic of Decision

### *Decision and Dreaming*
You decide your dream. Your dream might come to you or surface in you, but you decide if this is the dream you want and if you're going to pursue it.

### *Decision and Desire*
You decide what you want and what you desire. You can decide to stoke this desire or quelch it. If you decide to stoke your desires, you'll have a lot of drive to make what you want a reality.

### *Decision and Creativity*
Being creative is all about making choices and decisions. First, you decide to create something. Then, you decide what you want and what you want it to look or feel like. You also decide how to bring it into reality by reflecting on your authentic self.

### *Decision and the Moon Wheel*
You decide if you want to make a Moon Wheel and what you put into it. The Moon Wheel represents your life's sphere and your spirit's totality. Ultimately, you decide what your sphere of experience is going to be.

### *Decision and New Moon*
At the New Moon, you seed the Moon with your dreams and desires. You decide what those are.

### *Decision and First Quarter*
Decision seems to go hand in hand with action. Tony Robbins says, "All action is fathered by decision." When you decide what you want and that you're going to make it happen, the action becomes clear.

## Activating Lunar Alchemy

### *Decision and the Full Moon*
The Full Moon is an observation and self-reflection time. You decide to look. You decide what's meaningful to you or not. You can decide to see what's holding you back. You can decide what works for you.

### *Decision and Last Quarter*
The Last Quarter Moon is also a decision time. At the Last Quarter, you literally 'cut off' what's not working for you, what's obstructing you, and what's hurting you. The Last Quarter Moon is a very decisive moment in terms of choosing your dream, choosing what you want, and cutting off what's no longer supporting those aims.

### *Decision and Attention*
Your attention is a precious resource. It's considered one of the highest levels of brain function. You decide where to put your attention and what the most important things to attend to are.

### *Decision and Listening*
Listening is like tuning a radio. You can decide to expand your awareness of all the sounds, or you can decide to narrow your listening to one voice, as you would when you're having a conversation with a friend in a crowded and boisterous coffee shop. In many ways, you decide what you're listening for and how to respond.

## ACTIONS YOU CAN TAKE AS A RESULT OF READING THIS CHAPTER:

1. Decide what you want and what you're going to do to make it a reality for yourself.

2. Decide to practice Lunar Alchemy for three months.

3. Be deliberate in deciding how to use your precious and magical resources: desire, creativity, time, attention, and listening.

# About The Author

Reverend Sydney Francis is a teacher, writer, mystic and author of *Activating Lunar Alchemy*. Her 30-plus-year study and practice of art, astrology, healing, and the sacred mysteries illuminate her alchemical work with the Moon cycle and personal transformative practices.

Sydney has an MFA in Interdisciplinary Art from Goddard College, a Master's in Theology, and a Master's in Healing Arts from the Healing Light Center Church. She is an ordained minister, as well as a certified Wholeness Coach and emotional trauma healer.

She has received many awards for her dedication and creativity, including the Division of the Arts Prize, the Blodgett Scholarship,

## Activating Lunar Alchemy

and honors for her thesis and writing work. She also received an Honorarium for her innovative work on the *Children with Incarcerated Parents Study and Recommendations* from the University of Arizona, demonstrating her commitment and expertise in mental health and education to bring healing awareness in the wake of childhood emotional trauma.

Sydney lives, works, and writes in Sedona, AZ. Her day job includes creating mystical encounters for her guests at Sedona Esoteric Experiences. She enjoys slow Sundays with her husband and four children. For fun, she hikes in the Red Rocks with her dogs and two hiking cats and eats oversalted popcorn while savoring big-screen movies.

# Acknowledgements

There are many people to thank and acknowledge for their contribution to my life and the ideas behind *Activating Lunar Alchemy*. A book is by no means brought to life solely by the author. It takes a generous heaping of support, influence, and help from so many dedicated and amazing people.

My mom, Sondra Francis, told me throughout my life that I could do anything I set my mind to. She is an independent and self-made woman who hasn't let limitations get in her way. I'm eternally grateful to my mom for instilling in me this belief. If I didn't believe I could do anything I set my mind to, I wouldn't have believed I could have overcome my pain and obstacles, developed the Moon work practice, or written this book. One underlying principle of my work is a deeply held conviction that all things are possible. Thank you, mom!

## Activating Lunar Alchemy

Over the last few years since meeting my husband, Scott, this moon work has taken off. His interest in and practice of this moon work, as well as his love and support for me, have helped me to have confidence in myself and the value of this work. He has seen me through the ups and downs of becoming a first-time author: the enthusiasm for writing a book and the moments of self-doubt and fear. I'm grateful to Scott for being such a dedicated husband, companion, partner, friend and supporter.

I am so grateful and fortunate for my daughters, Sophia and Gemma. They have changed me and helped me grow. They have been there when I have struggled to balance single parenting with developing a creative idea. My daughters have shown me unconditional love, understanding and acceptance. Their lives have made mine so much richer.

In 2022, I married Scott and gained a very supportive extended family in Mark and Karin Scanlon, my father and mother-in-law, and my two stepchildren, Elizabeth and Scott Moore. These brilliant individuals are my family.

The body of this spiritual work owes a tremendous acknowledgement to the groundbreaking healing work of Reverend Rosalyn L. Bruyere and Ken Weintraub of the Healing Light Center Church. I found Reverend Rosalyn in 1995 as I was seeking a healing path for myself and others. I have learned so much from Rosalyn and Ken over these years, including energy healing, the Egyptian mysteries, and the Native American Medicine Wheel.

When I read through this book, I see the ideas, concepts and seeds that Reverend Rosalyn planted in my awareness. I also got ordained through the Healing Light Center Church's Crucible

## Acknowledgements

program, a dream I'm deeply honored and grateful to have been able to actualize. Thank you, Rosalyn and Ken, for the depth of healing and spiritual insight you share.

For the past four years, I have been teaching the Moon work and concepts in this book to a small group of devoted women. This group has helped me test and develop the practice of Lunar Alchemy. A special thank you to Angie Allen, Taz Chaudry, Barbara Ball, and Franchisca Rinaldi.

My friend, Michelle Tomburello, taught me to "seed the moon" almost 25 years ago. She also introduced me to the idea of planting intentions with a living plant to grow its energy over the years. Michelle has shared with me many magical and mystical insights and opened my mind to greater spiritual inquiry. I am thankful to Michelle for her friendship, intuition, and inspiration.

Another teacher who has changed my life with her knowledge and teaching is Astrologer Anne Ortelee. I learned about Anne in 2013 and began following her work. She has been my astrologer and teacher of astrology for many years. Her work in astrology has significantly influenced my understanding of astrological symbolism, timing, its cycles, and how to work with energy. Thank you, Anne.

In March of 2020, for my birthday, I participated in an extraordinary seminar called the Basic Seminar, presented by the Personal Success Institute (PSI). This seminar rocked my world and reminded me that my dream was to get ordained in the Healing Light Center's Crucible Program. Further study with PSI supported me to put this dream into action and overcome the subconscious obstacles that appeared to keep me limited and stuck. I'm so grateful to Renee Cermak, Portia Abrenica, Franchisca Rinaldi, and Amanda Beers.

## Activating Lunar Alchemy

Last, but by no means least, thank you to Natasa Denman and her inspired coaching work with the Ultimate 48-hour Author program. Her coaching, in addition to her extraordinary team, helped me break through the obstacles to writing this manuscript and overcome the challenges of publishing. Thank you also to Stuart Denman for his wise guidance and feedback in the structure and presentation of the book and to the publishing team of Vivienne Mason and Julie Fisher, who guided me through the publishing process. To my wonderful editor, Rebecca Low, who did a fantastic and efficient job of editing my book, I am so grateful for her ability and expertise. And thank you for the beautiful graphic work of Nik Boskovski for his gorgeous cover and diagram work.

# References

## Select Bibliography

Barbette Stanley Spaeth. (1996) 2010. *The Roman Goddess Ceres*. Univ of TX + ORM.

Barford, Eliot. 2013. "Biological Clocks Defy Circadian Rhythms." *Nature*, September. https://doi.org/10.1038/nature.2013.13833.

Boyle, Rebecca. 2024. *Our Moon*. Sceptre.

Bruyere, Rosalyn L. 1994. *Wheels of Light: Chakras, Auras, and the Healing Energy of the Body*. New York: Fireside Book.

Cajochen, Christian, Songül Altanay-Ekici, Mirjam Münch, Sylvia Frey, Vera Knoblauch, and Anna Wirz-Justice. 2013. "Evidence That the Lunar Cycle Influences Sleep." *Current Biology* 23 (15): 1485–88. https://doi.org/10.1016/j.cub.2013.06.029.

Casey, Caroline. (1998) 2013. *Making the Gods Work for You*. New York: Harmony Books.

Fell, Andy. 2018. "How the Moon Formed inside a Vaporized Earth Synestia." UC Davis. February 28, 2018. https://www.ucdavis.edu/news/how-moon-formed-inside-vaporized-earth-synestia.

Fortune, Dion. 1935. *The Mystical Qabalah*. Red Wheel.

Harper, Douglas. 2023. "Online Etymology Dictionary." Etymonline.com. 2023. https://www.etymonline.com/.

Hill, Napoleon. (1937) 2019. *Think and Grow Rich*. S.L.: Simon & Brown.

———. 2021. *Outwitting the Devil*. Sound Wisdom.

International Association for the Study of Pain (IASP). 2020a. "IASP Announces Revised Definition of Pain." International Association for the Study of Pain (IASP). July 16, 2020. https://www.iasp-pain.org/publications/iasp-news/iasp-announces-revised-definition-of-pain/.

———. 2020b. "IASP Announces Revised Definition of Pain." International Association for the Study of Pain (IASP). July 16, 2020. https://www.iasp-pain.org/publications/iasp-news/iasp-announces-revised-definition-of-pain/.

LaPorte, Danielle. 2014. *Desire Map Workbook*. Sounds True Adult.

Lotzof, Kerry. n.d. "How Does the Moon Affect Life on Earth?" Www.nhm.ac.uk. Accessed January 20, 2024. https://www.nhm.ac.uk/discover/how-does-the-moon-affect-life-on-earth.html.

Paul Foster Case. (1947) 2006. *The Tarot: A Key to the Wisdom of the Ages*. New York: Jeremy P. Tarcher/Penguin.

Spiller, Jan. (2001) 2007. *New Moon Astrology*. Bantam.

Walter, Chip. 2009. *Thumbs, Toes, and Tears*. Bloomsbury Publishing USA.

Williams, Carol. 1998. *Bringing a Garden to Life*. Bantam.

Wright, Machaelle Small. 1987. *Perelandra Garden Workbook*. Perelandra, Limited.

Wright, Machaelle S. 1990. *Perelandra Garden Workbook II*. Perelandra, Limited.

# 2 Offers With Calls To Action

### *Lunar Alchemy Quick Start Key*

You're ready to get started with *Activating Lunar Alchemy*, but you're short on time and apprehensive about diving in fully. Are you looking for a quick and effective way to start attuning to the Moon cycle? Do you prefer the ease and efficiency of a workbook to create your own Moon Wheels? Or perhaps you want to download the diagrams from the book as your key to unlocking the mystery of *Activating Lunar Alchemy*.

- Discover how to make the magic work for you
- Unlock your key to flourishing

## Activating Lunar Alchemy

- Access these potent tools for your success
- Work smarter with the Moon's timing
- Transmute your emotional pain into spiritual abundance

Download the Quick Start Key here: https://thesydneyfrancis.com/products/key

## The Essential Lunar Alchemy Course

Have you recently been through a major transition, such as a divorce, loss, or career change? Your life is in the flux and instability of change. You're seeking to regain stability, gather a sense of balance, and get your bearings as you figure out what's next. You want to relieve the pain of loss, find your spiritual center, and feel more guided.

I've been there. I got a divorce in 2012, and my life was turned upside down in every way. I utilized this Moon work to set the course toward my dreams, to give me emotional stability and rhythm, and to help me navigate and heal from the painful loss of divorce. Although my divorce was a very difficult chapter in my life, it taught me so much about myself, what I wanted, and how to be more responsible for my life and my dreams.

If you're seeking a weekly spiritual practice that can help you regain stability, balance, clarity, and direction, *The Essential Lunar Alchemy* is for you. In this six-week course, you'll learn to attune to the Moon's rhythm through weekly Moon Wheels for healing change and increased spiritual connection. As a bonus, you'll receive weekly access to a live Moon work group, where I will guide and support you through your healing journey with the Moon.

## 2 Offers With Calls To Action

Are you ready to transmute your emotional pain into spiritual abundance?

- Connect with the magic of the Moon
- Regain balance and wholeness
- Unlock the mystery of unconscious patterns that are holding you back
- Leverage your creativity to create the life of your dreams
- Learn the secrets of Alchemy and Transmutation to positively change your life

Get access now! Go to https://thesydneyfrancis.com/products/essential

# SYDNEY FRANCIS

### Applied Alchemy: Transform Your Life
- How to Apply Alchemical Mysteries to Transform Your Life
- Access Your Potentiality & Make it a Reality
- Learn the Secrets of Transmutation Utilizing the Moon's Rhythm

### The Magic of the Moon
- Connect with the Magic of the Moon
- Unlock the Mystery of Unconscious Patterns that are Holding You Back
- Attune to Divine Timing in Order to Flourish

### Leverage Your Creativity
- Live the Life of Your Dreams by Applying Simple Creative Tools
- Access Your Higher Potential
- Learn the Secrets to Directing and Optimizing Your Energy

Reverend Sydney Francis is an instructor, writer, spiritual leader, and author of *Activating Lunar Alchemy*. Her 30-plus-year study and practice of art, astrology, healing, and the sacred mysteries illuminate her alchemical work with the Moon cycle and personal transformative practices.

Sydney has an MFA in Interdisciplinary Art from Goddard College, a Master's in Theology, and a Master's in Healing Arts from the Healing Light Center Church. She is an ordained minister, as well as a certified Wholeness Coach and emotional trauma healer.

As a former University Instructor, Sydney has presented many lectures and classes and facilitated groups across the Southwestern US and online.

---

Contact Reverend Sydney today to schedule a presentation.
✉ sydney@sedonaesotericexperiences.com  ☏ 928-864-7060  🌐 www.sedonaesotericexperiences.com

# End Notes

## Chapter 2: The Magic of the Moon

[1] Boyle, Rebecca. *Our Moon*, Random House LLC (New York, NY: 2024).

[2] Lotzof, Kerry. n.d. "How Does the Moon Affect Life on Earth?" Www.nhm.ac.uk. Accessed January 20, 2024. https://www.nhm.ac.uk/discover/how-does-the-moon-affect-life-on-earth.html.

[3] "Transmutation." Merriam-Webster.com Thesaurus, Merriam-Webster, https://www.merriam-webster.com/thesaurus/transmutation. Accessed 25 Jan. 2024.

[4] Boyle, Rebecca. "The Creation," *Our Moon*, Random House LLC (New York, NY: 2024).

[5] Fell, Andy. 2018. "How the Moon Formed inside a Vaporized Earth Synestia." UC Davis. February 28, 2018. https://www.ucdavis.edu/news/how-moon-formed-inside-vaporized-earth-synestia.

[6] Barford, Eliot. 2013. "Biological Clocks Defy Circadian Rhythms." *Nature*, September. https://doi.org/10.1038/nature.2013.13833.

[7] Cajochen, Christian, Songül Altanay-Ekici, Mirjam Münch, Sylvia Frey, Vera Knoblauch, and Anna Wirz-Justice. 2013. "Evidence That the Lunar Cycle Influences Sleep." *Current Biology* 23 (15): 1485–88. https://doi.org/10.1016/j.cub.2013.06.029.

[8] Barford, Eliot. 2013. "Biological Clocks Defy Circadian Rhythms." *Nature*, September. https://doi.org/10.1038/nature.2013.13833

## Chapter 3: The Magic of Dreaming

[9] "Dream | Etymology, Origin and Meaning of Dream by Etymonline." n.d. Www.etymonline.com. https://www.etymonline.com/word/dream#etymonline_v_15895.

## Chapter 4: The Magic of Desire

[10] Harper, Douglas. 2021. "Desire | Etymology of Desire by Etymonline." Www.etymonline.com. October 13, 2021. https://www.etymonline.com/word/desire#etymonline_v_5657.

## Chapter 5: The Magic of Creativity

[11] Walter, Chip. Thumbs, Toes, and Tears: And Other Traits That Make Us Human, Walker & Company, New York, Copyright: 2006

[12] *Creative Arts: Enhancing mental health and well-being.* (n.d.). https://www.psychiatry.org/news-room/apa-blogs/creative-arts-enhancing-mental-health#:~:text=Creative%20arts%20are%20used%20in,drawing%2C%20painting%20and%20craft%20therapy.

[13] *creativity | Etymology of creativity by etymonline.* (n.d.). Online Etymology Dictionary. https://www.etymonline.com/word/creativity#etymonline_v_36301. Accessed January 4, 2024

# End Notes

## Chapter 11: The Magic of Attention

[14] Lindsay GW (2020) Attention in Psychology, Neuroscience, and Machine Learning. *Front. Comput. Neurosci.* 14:29. doi: 10.3389/fncom.2020.00029

[15] Lindsay GW (2020) Attention in Psychology, Neuroscience, and Machine Learning. *Front. Comput. Neurosci.* 14:29. doi: 10.3389/fncom.2020.00029

[16] "Brain focus and concentration problems", Life Focus https://lifeseasons.com/glossary/brain-focus-and-concentration-problems/#:~:text=BRAIN%20FOCUS%20&%20CONCENTRATION%20FACTS%20&%20STATISTICS&text=The%20human%20brain%20is%20able,about%206%20hours%20a%20week.

[17] Lindsay GW (2020) Attention in Psychology, Neuroscience, and Machine Learning. *Front. Comput. Neurosci.* 14:29. doi: 10.3389/fncom.2020.00029

[18] "Brain focus and concentration problems", Life Focus https://lifeseasons.com/glossary/brain-focus-and-concentration-problems/#:~:text=BRAIN%20FOCUS%20&%20CONCENTRATION%20FACTS%20&%20STATISTICS&text=The%20human%20brain%20is%20able,about%206%20hours%20a%20week.

## Chapter 12: The Magic of Listening

[19] Harper, Douglas. "Etymology of listen." Online Etymology Dictionary, https://www.etymonline.com/word/listen. Accessed 24 December 2023.

## Chapter 13: The Magic of Decision

[20] https://www.etymonline.com/word/decide#etymonline_v_852

# Notes

## Activating Lunar Alchemy

# Notes

# Activating Lunar Alchemy

# Notes

www.ingramcontent.com/pod-product-compliance
Lightning Source LLC
Chambersburg PA
CBHW030037100526
44590CB00011B/235